THE MEGABOOK OF SPELLING

WILEY BLEVINS

GRADES K–2

Ready-to-Use Templates and Activities to Boost Phonics Lessons

Supports the Science of Reading

📖 **SCHOLASTIC**

Excepting those parts intended for classroom use, no part of this publication may be reproduced in whole or in part, or stored in a retrieval system, or transmitted in any form or by any means, electronic, mechanical, photocopying, recording, or otherwise, or used to train any artificial intelligence technologies, without the express written permission of the publisher. For information regarding permission, write to Scholastic Inc., 557 Broadway, New York, NY 10012. Scholastic Inc. grants teachers who have purchased this product permission to reproduce from this book those pages intended for use in their classrooms. Notice of copyright must appear on all copies of copyrighted materials.

SVP & Publisher: Tara Welty
Editor: Maria L. Chang
Cover design: Tannaz Fassihi
Interior design: Michelle H. Kim
Illustrations: Rob McClurkan; Doug Jones; Abby Carter; Jackie Snider; Shutterstock Inc.; Noun Project

ISBN: 978-1-5461-5254-5
Scholastic Inc., 557 Broadway, New York, NY 10012
Copyright © 2025 by Wiley Blevins
Published by Scholastic Inc. All rights reserved.
Printed in the U.S.A.
First printing, March 2025
1 2 3 4 5 6 7 8 9 10   207   34 33 32 31 30 29 28 27 26 25

TABLE OF CONTENTS

INTRODUCTION: GUIDING PRINCIPLES 4

SECTION 1: SOUND BOXES 6

SECTION 2: DICTATION 78

SECTION 3: CUMULATIVE SPELLING SENTENCES 98

SECTION 4: WORD-BUILDING CHAINS 108

SECTION 5: WORD-SORT SETS 128

SECTION 6: WORD-BUILDING CENTER 143

SECTION 7: TEACH PHONICS TO MASTERY: SCOPE AND SEQUENCE 217

SECTION 8: WRITE ABOUT DECODABLE TEXTS 224

SECTION 9: SYNTAX: BUILDING COMPLEX SENTENCES 244

SECTION 10: STUDENT WRITING EVALUATION TOOLS FOR WRITER'S NOTEBOOK 254

SECTION 11: IRREGULAR HIGH-FREQUENCY WORDS 261

SECTION 12: HANDWRITING FLUENCY 287

SECTION 13: RULES AND GENERALIZATIONS 315

INTRODUCTION

Guiding Principles

Spelling is an essential part of phonics instruction. Too often phonics lessons contain an imbalance between the decoding (reading) work and the encoding (writing) work. Every phonics lesson must include an encoding activity—such as dictation, word building, or writing about decodable texts—in which children must use their newly taught phonics skills in spelling words with those same skills. Generally, children can read words with taught phonics skills before they can spell them. As a result, spelling requires more time and intentionality in our instruction. This intensive focus on transferring phonics skills to writing will also deepen children's understanding of how our English writing system works. The following guiding principles are designed to accelerate children's use of phonics patterns in their writing and meet the wide range of individual child needs present in most classrooms.

6 Key Principles of Spelling Instruction During Phonics Lessons

Principle 1: Phonemic Awareness (Oral Segmentation)

Children need to be able to orally segment words into their individual sounds to spell them. When children learn to spell words, they must attend to each sound in a word and attach a letter or spelling to that sound. Over time, these spellings are stored in a child's memory. Oral segmentation activities can involve tapping sounds, chopping sounds, counting sounds with fingers held up, and using Elkonin (sound) boxes to physically mark sounds with counters. These activities are more beneficial when they include letters. For example, children can mark the sounds in a word in the sound boxes using counters (or marking a dot), then immediately replace each counter with the letter or spelling that represents that sound in writing.

Principle 2: Phonics and Handwriting Fluency

To spell well, children must learn the most frequent spellings for each sound in English. This is accomplished through explicit phonics instruction in the first few years of school. It takes longer for children to transfer spellings into writing than reading, so more focus and continued focus will be needed well past the initial introduction of a phonics skill. Simultaneously, children need to develop handwriting fluency—the automatic formation of letters. Activities in kindergarten in which children practice writing the letters as they say the letter's most common sound can accelerate and solidify this learning. Teachers typically review letter-sounds briefly at the beginnings of lessons using letter and spelling cards. Children see the letter or spelling and chorally state the sound. The reverse should also happen as a daily warm-up. The teacher should say a sound and ask children to write the letter or spelling (sometimes multiple spellings) for that sound. The teacher can reinforce proper letter formation during this activity and provide articulation support. Some children struggle with where to start forming a letter and how to correctly form it.

Principle 3: Print Exposure Through Decodable Texts

In the early grades, use decodable texts (in which a high percentage of the words contain taught phonics patterns) to build fluency reading words with these patterns. These repeated readings have an additional benefit: Seeing these patterns in many words over and over builds statistical awareness of how these spelling patterns are used in words and can accelerate children's awareness of and use of these patterns when writing.

Principle 4: Daily Spelling and Writing Activities

Children should engage in encoding (spelling/writing) activities every day and in every phonics lesson. It takes longer to transfer these patterns to writing than reading. These activities can vary, each with an important instructional focus. These include dictation (guided spelling of letters, words, and simple sentences), word building (using letter cards or magnetic letters to manipulate sounds and spellings in a series of words), word sorts (with discussions about key spelling observations that can aid in writing), writing about decodable texts (an application of skills activity that also checks comprehension), and so on. Extra attention must also be afforded to the irregular high-frequency words (e.g., *said, was, they*) that many children struggle to spell because of their irregular or less-common spelling patterns.

Principle 5: Focus on How English Works

Some languages, such as Spanish, are more "transparent." That means there is a high degree of consistency between the letter or spelling and the sound it represents. However, English is a language that is less transparent. We refer to it as an "opaque" language. While there are many letters and spellings that consistently stand for a sound, there are sounds in English that can be represented by many letters or spellings. For example, we can write *e, ee, ea, ie, ei, y,* and *ey* for the long-*e* sound. This opaqueness requires us to spend MORE time for instruction and practice on these spellings with our students and MORE attention to when and why these spellings are used in words. So, effective spelling instruction includes observations, discussions, and explicit explanations about how English words work. While teaching a vast array of rules is not helpful, there are a handful of rules and generalizations (e.g., no English words end in the letter *v* so you must add an *e*) that are worth teaching children. In addition, a deeper focus on related words can reveal the morphophonemic quality of English and how spellings are maintained across related words. For example, the related words *sign, signal,* and *signature,* which all contain "sign," help children understand why that "silent" *g* is necessary in the word *sign*. Also, some children speak a variation of mainstream English (e.g., African American English, Chicano English) or a regional dialect that pose some complexities when children are spelling words due to modified or dropped sounds. All these require direct instruction and support.

Principle 6: Assessment and Differentiated Supports

Children in any given classroom represent a range of mastery in terms of spelling. Therefore, it is necessary to assess spelling in a cumulative manner, monitor spelling whole class and individually, and provide differentiated supports. This makes teaching spelling more challenging and complex for teachers. Simple assessment structures and tools (provided here) and differentiated activities go a long way to better meet all children's spelling needs.

INTRODUCTION

HOW TO USE THIS BOOK

1. Set aside 5–10 minutes each day during whole- and small-group to add spelling activities.

2. Select a variety of activities each week, creating a pattern (e.g., Monday sound boxes, Tuesday word building, Wednesday dictation, Thursday write about decodable text, Friday dictation).

3. Use the other activities for independent and center-time work (e.g., handwriting fluency, word-building centers).

4. You can also send these activities home for additional practice.

Principle 1: Phonemic Awareness (Oral Segmentation)

Skills Practiced

Phonemic Awareness

Handwriting

Spelling

Decoding

Dictation

Writing

Section 1 downloadables are available here.

SECTION 1

Sound Boxes

To spell words, children need to be able to orally segment words into their individual sounds. When learning to spell words, children must attend to each sound in a word and attach a letter or spelling to that sound. Over time, these spellings are stored in a child's memory. Oral segmentation activities can involve tapping sounds, chopping sounds, counting sounds with fingers held up, and using Elkonin (sound) boxes to physically mark sounds with counters. These activities are more beneficial when they include letters. For example, children can mark the sounds in a word in the sound boxes using counters (or marking a dot), then immediately replace each counter with the letter or spelling that represents that sound in writing.

Multimodal and Multisensory Supports

When segmenting by sounds, use tapping, sound boxes, and color cards for children who need additional support. Holding up one finger for each sound is especially beneficial (and provides more support than tapping). In this way, there is a record of the number of sounds counted in a word. Wiggle your finger for the first sound, ask what it is, then guide children to write the letter or spelling for that sound. Continue in this manner for the rest of the word. These are effective ways to modify a whole-group lesson or for use during small-group time.

When segmenting by syllables, teach children the "chin drop" technique. Have them place their hands underneath their chins and count the number of times their chin drops (vowel sounds) as they say the word. Remind children that each syllable has one vowel sound. Then, have children write one syllable at a time.

Materials Needed	The following pages provide guided practice in segmenting sounds in words, then attaching a letter or spelling to each sound. • Pages 12–28 feature consonant sounds and prompt children to distinguish whether the sound appears in the beginning (initial position) or ending (final position) of a word. • Pages 29–57 provide full segmentation and writing of simple one-syllable words. • Pages 58–77 focus on spelling multisyllabic words one syllable at a time and use syllable boxes instead of sound boxes. **Optional:** Counters (up to five for each child to use with the sound boxes)
Length of Activity	3–5 minutes
Location	school or home

Note: See pages 9–11 for an image answer key that provides each picture name for clarity.

Phonemic Awareness Routine

Use the following phonemic awareness routine for oral segmentation.

Routine Steps	Sample Teacher Talk
Step 1: Introduce Tell children the purpose of the activity.	*Today we will be segmenting, or taking apart, a word sound by sound.*
Step 2: Model (I Do) Model how to segment the sounds in a word. Use sound boxes (Elkonin boxes) and counters. Start with two-letter words (e.g., *am, is*), progress to CVC words (e.g., *sat, man*) starting with continuous sounds that can be stretched (e.g., /f/, /l/, /m/, /n/, /r/, /s/, /v/, /z/), progress to words that begin with stop sounds (e.g., *bag*), and then progress to words beginning with consonant blends (e.g., *slip*), and so on.	*I am going to say a word, then I will say it sound by sound. As I say each sound, I will place one counter in each box. Listen:* **sat**. *Say:* **sat**. *Now I will say* **sat** *sound by sound* [stretch each sound three seconds so children can hear each discrete sound]: */sss/* [place counter in first box], */aaa/* [place counter in second box], */t/* [place counter in third box]. *The word* **sat** *has three sounds: /s/, /a/, /t/.* [Point to each box as you say the sound.]
Step 3: Guided Practice (We Do, You Do) State words (as many as time permits) for children to segment phoneme by phoneme, or sound by sound. Do the first word with children. Use sound (Elkonin) boxes as a support early on. You can use sound boxes for CVC words, short-vowel words with consonant blends and digraphs, and even some simple long-vowel words. However, as spellings become more complex, such as words with a final *e*, the boxes will be less clear-cut, and children should have enough experience segmenting words to not need them for all oral activities. You can continue using them during dictation as needed. **Corrective Feedback:** When children make mistakes, stretch the word using the rubber-band technique (pretend you are holding an imaginary rubber band and stretch it as you stretch the sounds) or chopping technique (stretch the sounds as you chop with your hands together as you move from sound to sound). Have children repeat. Then, use the sound boxes to model how to place one counter on each box as you stretch the word and move from sound to sound. Repeat the routine using the same word, asking children to respond without you.	*Listen to the word. Segment, or break apart, the word sound by sound.*

SECTION 1
Sound Boxes

Routine Steps (continued)	Sample Teacher Talk (continued)
Step 4: Connect to Spelling Use segmentation and the sound boxes to help children transition to spelling words. After children have segmented a word, have them replace each counter with a letter (or letters) to spell the word. This breaking apart and then putting together of words using printed letters will accelerate children's understanding of how words work.	*Now that we've taken apart the word sound by sound, let's rebuild the word letter by letter.* *What is the first sound you hear in* **sat**? [Pause for children to answer.] *That's right, the first sound in* **sat** *is /s/. What letter do we write when we hear the /s/ sound?* [Pause for children to answer.] *That's right, we write the letter* **s**. *Replace your counter in the first box with the letter* **s**. [Continue in the same way with the rest of the word. For children who need support, stretch the sounds in the word as you tap on each box. Ask children to listen for the sound in the target box, such as the middle box, as you say the sound.]

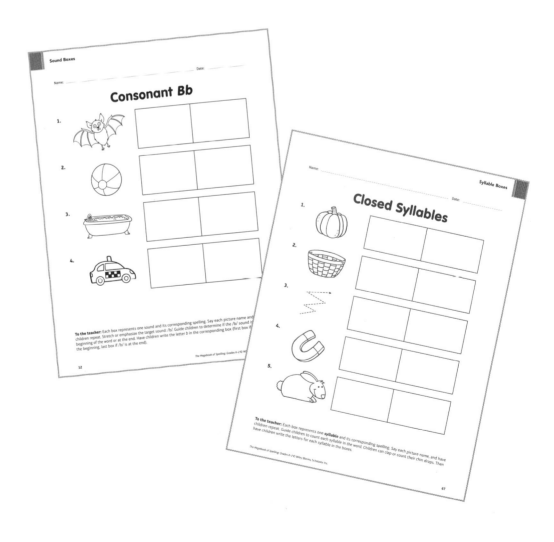

The Megabook of Spelling: Grades K–2

Sound Box: Image Answer Key

Consonant *Bb* (page 12)
1. bat 2. ball 3. tub 4. cab

Consonant *Dd* (page 13)
1. dog 2. bed 3. sad 4. dinosaur

Consonant *Ff* (page 14)
1. fish 2. fan 3. leaf 4. flower

Consonant *Gg* (page 15)
1. girl 2. bug 3. leg 4. goat

Consonant *Ll* (page 16)
1. leaf 2. seal 3. lips 4. leg

Consonant *Mm* (page 17)
1. man 2. moon 3. mop 4. drum

Consonant *Nn* (page 18)
1. nose 2. fan 3. bone 4. nail

Consonant *Pp* (page 19)
1. pig 2. cup 3. pencil 4. map

Consonant *Ss* (page 20)
1. sun 2. bus 3. sit 4. sandwich

Consonant *Tt* (page 21)
1. ten 2. hat 3. boat 4. tie

Consonant *Cc*, Digraph *ck* (page 22)
1. cat 2. cup 3. rock 4. sock

Consonants *Hh, Jj* (page 23)
1. hat 2. jump 3. jellyfish 4. heart

Consonants *Kk, Rr* (page 24)
1. rug 2. kiss 3. run 4. kit

Consonants *Vv, Ww* (page 25)
1. window 2. worm 3. vet 4. van

Consonants *Yy, Zz* (page 26)
1. zebra 2. yo-yo 3. yell 4. zipper

Consonant *Xx* (page 27)
1. box 2. six 3. fox 4. mix

Consonant *Qq* (*qu*) (page 28)
1. queen 2. quilt 3. question 4. quiet

Short *a* (page 29)
1. sad 2. mad 3. cat 4. bat 5. fan

Short *i* (page 30)
1. sit 2. big 3. fin 4. chin 5. zip

Short *o* (page 31)
1. mop 2. hot 3. dog 4. sock 5. rock

Short *u* (page 32)
1. sun 2. bus 3. rug 4. jump 5. nuts

Short *e* (page 33)
1. vet 2. ten 3. leg 4. sled 5. desk

Consonant Blends (*l*-blends) (page 34)
1. lip 2. slip 3. clap 4. block 5. plant

Consonant Blends (*s*-blends) (page 35)
1. top 2. stop 3. smell 4. swim 5. skunk

Consonant Blends (*r*-blends) (page 36)
1. cab 2. crab 3. grass 4. dress 5. bread

Digraph *sh* (page 37)
1. ship 2. shell 3. fish 4. brush 5. trash

Digraph *th* (page 38)
1. thin 2. thick 3. bath 4. moth 5. math

Digraph *ch*, Trigraph *tch* (page 39)
1. chin 2. chick 3. catch 4. witch 5. bench

SECTION 1
Sound Boxes

SECTION 1
Sound Boxes

Digraph wh (page 40)
1. When 2. Which 3. Why 4. Where 5. white

Digraph ng, Blend nk (page 41)
1. king 2. ring 3. sink 4. drink 5. string

Final e (page 42)
1. five 2. rope 3. vase 4. bike 5. cube

Long a (page 43)
1. rain 2. train 3. chain 4. pay 5. tray

Long e (page 44)
1. leaf 2. read 3. sheep 4. sleep 5. street

Long o (page 45)
1. boat 2. soap 3. snow 4. blow 5. throw

Long i (page 46)
1. light 2. night 3. pie 4. fly 5. cry

Long u (page 47)
1. cube 2. few 3. menu 4. huge 5. (Teacher's choice)

r-Controlled Vowels er, ir, ur (page 48)
1. bird 2. girl 3. first 4. surf 5. teacher

r-Controlled Vowel ar (page 49)
1. car 2. barn 3. park 4. star 5. shark

r-Controlled Vowels or, ore, oor, our (page 50)
1. door 2. floor 3. horse 4. store 5. four

r-Controlled Vowels air, ear, are (page 51)
1. chair 2. stairs 3. bear 4. pear 5. share

Diphthongs oi, oy (page 52)
1. boy 2. toys 3. boil 4. soil 5. point

Diphthongs ou, ow (page 53)
1. house 2. shout 3. town 4. down 5. clown

Complex Vowel /ô/ a(l), au, aw (page 54)
1. ball 2. small 3. claw 4. straw 5. walk

Short oo (page 55)
1. book 2. hook 3. hood 4. cook 5. foot

Long oo (oo, ew, ue, oe) (page 56)
1. moon 2. spoon 3. shoe 4. glue 5. new

Silent Letters (page 57)
1. knob 2. knit 3. knock 4. write 5. sign

Prefixes un-, re- (page 58)
1. unlock 2. unwrap 3. recook 4. reread 5. recycle

Suffix -ing (page 59)
1. jumping 2. sleeping 3. eating 4. washing 5. playing

Suffix -ed (page 60)
1. planted 2. listed 3. landed 4. lifted 5. melted

Suffixes -ful, -less (page 61)
1. helpful 2. graceful 3. fearless 4. hopeless 5. thankful

SECTION 1
Sound Boxes

Suffixes *-y*, *-ly* (page 62)
1. hairy 2. itchy 3. messy
4. sadly 5. friendly

Final Stable Syllables
(*tion*, *sion*, *ture*, *sure*) (page 63)
1. picture 2. treasure 3. vulture
4. question 5. explosion

Compound Words (page 64)
1. hotdog 2. cupcake
3. snowman 4. toothbrush 5. butterfly

Compound Words (page 65)
1. airplane 2. birdhouse 3. bathtub
4. football 5. sunflower

Closed Syllables (page 66)
1. kitten 2. pencil
3. sandwich 4. cactus 5. insect

Closed Syllables (page 67)
1. pumpkin 2. basket 3. zigzag
4. magnet 5. rabbit

Open Syllables (page 68)
1. baby 2. frozen 3. minus
4. photo 5. zebra

Open Syllables (page 69)
1. table 2. silent 3. pilot
4. music 5. diver

r-Controlled Vowel Syllables (page 70)
1. doctor 2. ladder 3. turkey 4. forty
5. circus

r-Controlled Vowel Syllables (page 71)
1. artist 2. tractor 3. finger 4. garden
5. monster

Vowel Team Syllables (page 72)
1. railroad 2. highway 3. thirteen
4. monkey 5. mushroom

Vowel Team Syllables (page 73)
1. scarecrow 2. donkey
3. flashlight 4. fifteen 5. mermaid

Consonant + *le* Syllables (page 74)
1. table 2. candle 3. puzzle 4. turtle
5. circle

Consonant + *le* Syllables (page 75)
1. bottle 2. bubble 3. saddle
4. apple 5. eagle

Final-*e* Syllables (page 76)
1. inside 2. escape 3. mistake
4. tadpole 5. reptile

Final-*e* Syllables (page 77)
1. outside 2. trombone 3. erase
4. explode 5. athlete

Sound Boxes

Name: _____ Date: _____

Consonant Bb

1.

2.

3.

4.

To the teacher: Each box represents one sound and its corresponding spelling. Say each picture name and have children repeat. Stretch or emphasize the target sound: /b/. Guide children to determine if the /b/ sound is at the beginning of the word or at the end. Have children write the letter *b* in the corresponding box (first box if /b/ is at the beginning, last box if /b/ is at the end).

The Megabook of Spelling: Grades K–2 © Wiley Blevins, Scholastic Inc.

Sound Boxes

Name: _____ Date: _____

Consonant Dd

1.

2.

3.

4.

To the teacher: Each box represents one sound and its corresponding spelling. Say each picture name and have children repeat. Stretch or emphasize the target sound: /d/. Guide children to determine if the /d/ sound is at the beginning of the word or at the end. Have children write the letter *d* in the corresponding box (first box if /d/ is at the beginning, last box if /d/ is at the end).

Sound Boxes

Name: _____ Date: _____

Consonant Ff

1.

2.

3.

4.

To the teacher: Each box represents one sound and its corresponding spelling. Say each picture name and have children repeat. Stretch or emphasize the target sound: /f/. Guide children to determine if the /f/ sound is at the beginning of the word or at the end. Have children write the letter *f* in the corresponding box (first box if /f/ is at the beginning, last box if /f/ is at the end).

Sound Boxes

Name: _____ Date: _____

Consonant Gg

1.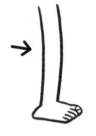

2.

3.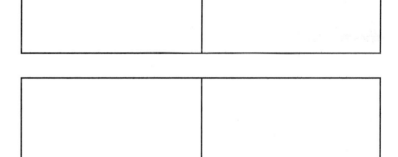

4.

To the teacher: Each box represents one sound and its corresponding spelling. Say each picture name and have children repeat. Stretch or emphasize the target sound: /g/. Guide children to determine if the /g/ sound is at the beginning of the word or at the end. Have children write the letter g in the corresponding box (first box if /g/ is at the beginning, last box if /g/ is at the end).

The Megabook of Spelling: Grades K–2 © Wiley Blevins, Scholastic Inc.

15

Sound Boxes

Name: _____   Date: _____

Consonant Ll

1.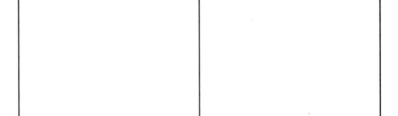

2.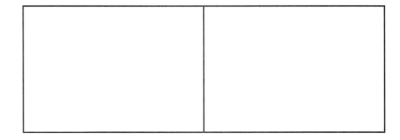

3.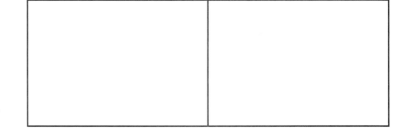

4.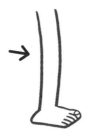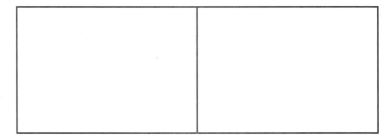

To the teacher: Each box represents one sound and its corresponding spelling. Say each picture name and have children repeat. Stretch or emphasize the target sound: /l/. Guide children to determine if the /l/ sound is at the beginning of the word or at the end. Have children write the letter *l* in the corresponding box (first box if /l/ is at the beginning, last box if /l/ is at the end).

Sound Boxes

Name: _____ Date: _____

Consonant Mm

1.
2.
3.
4.

To the teacher: Each box represents one sound and its corresponding spelling. Say each picture name and have children repeat. Stretch or emphasize the target sound: /m/. Guide children to determine if the /m/ sound is at the beginning of the word or at the end. Have children write the letter *m* in the corresponding box (first box if /m/ is at the beginning, last box if /m/ is at the end).

The Megabook of Spelling: Grades K–2 © Wiley Blevins, Scholastic Inc.

Sound Boxes

Name: _____   Date: _____

Consonant Nn

1.

2.

3.

4.

To the teacher: Each box represents one sound and its corresponding spelling. Say each picture name and have children repeat. Stretch or emphasize the target sound: /n/. Guide children to determine if the /n/ sound is at the beginning of the word or at the end. Have children write the letter *n* in the corresponding box (first box if /n/ is at the beginning, last box if /n/ is at the end).

Sound Boxes

Name: _____ Date: _____

Consonant Pp

1.

2.

3.

4.

To the teacher: Each box represents one sound and its corresponding spelling. Say each picture name and have children repeat. Stretch or emphasize the target sound: /p/. Guide children to determine if the /p/ sound is at the beginning of the word or at the end. Have children write the letter p in the corresponding box (first box if /p/ is at the beginning, last box if /p/ is at the end).

The Megabook of Spelling: Grades K–2 © Wiley Blevins, Scholastic Inc.

Sound Boxes

Name: _____ Date: _____

Consonant Ss

1.

2.

3.

4.

To the teacher: Each box represents one sound and its corresponding spelling. Say each picture name and have children repeat. Stretch or emphasize the target sound: /s/. Guide children to determine if the /s/ sound is at the beginning of the word or at the end. Have children write the letter s in the corresponding box (first box if /s/ is at the beginning, last box if /s/ is at the end).

The Megabook of Spelling: Grades K–2 © Wiley Blevins, Scholastic Inc.

Sound Boxes

Name: _____ Date: _____

Consonant Tt

1.

2.

3.

4.

To the teacher: Each box represents one sound and its corresponding spelling. Say each picture name and have children repeat. Stretch or emphasize the target sound: /t/. Guide children to determine if the /t/ sound is at the beginning of the word or at the end. Have children write the letter *t* in the corresponding box (first box if /t/ is at the beginning, last box if /t/ is at the end).

The Megabook of Spelling: Grades K–2 © Wiley Blevins, Scholastic Inc.

Sound Boxes

Name: _____ Date: _____

Consonant Cc, Digraph ck

1.

2.

3.

4.

To the teacher: Each box represents one sound and its corresponding spelling. Say each picture name and have children repeat. Stretch or emphasize the target sound: /k/. Guide children to determine if the /k/ sound is at the beginning of the word or at the end. Have children write the letter *c* in the first box (if /k/ is at the beginning) or *ck* in the last box (if /k/ is at the end).

The Megabook of Spelling: Grades K–2 © Wiley Blevins, Scholastic Inc.

Sound Boxes

Name: _____   Date: _____

Consonants Hh, Jj

1.

2.

3.

4.

To the teacher: Each box represents one sound and its corresponding spelling. Say each picture name and have children repeat. Stretch or emphasize the target sounds: /h/ and /j/. Guide children to write the letter *h* or *j* in the first box based on the sound they hear at the beginning of the word—/h/ or /j/.

The Megabook of Spelling: Grades K–2 © Wiley Blevins, Scholastic Inc.

Sound Boxes

Name: _____ Date: _____

Consonants Kk, Rr

1.

2.

3.

4.

To the teacher: Each box represents one sound and its corresponding spelling. Say each picture name and have children repeat. Stretch or emphasize the target sounds: /k/ and /r/. Guide children to write the letter *k* or *r* in the first box based on the sound they hear at the beginning of the word—/k/ or /r/.

Sound Boxes

Name: _____ Date: _____

Consonants Vv, Ww

1.

2.

3.

4.

To the teacher: Each box represents one sound and its corresponding spelling. Say each picture name and have children repeat. Stretch or emphasize the target sounds: /v/ and /w/. Guide children to write the letter v or w in the first box based on the sound they hear at the beginning of the word—/v/ or /w/.

The Megabook of Spelling: Grades K–2 © Wiley Blevins, Scholastic Inc.

Sound Boxes

Name: _____ Date: _____

Consonants Yy, Zz

1.

2.

3.

4.

To the teacher: Each box represents one sound and its corresponding spelling. Say each picture name and have children repeat. Stretch or emphasize the target sounds: /y/ and /z/. Guide children to write the letter y or z in the first box based on the sound they hear at the beginning of the word—/y/ or /z/.

Sound Boxes

Name: _____   Date: _____

Consonant Xx

1.

2.

3.

4.

To the teacher: Say each picture name and have children repeat. Stretch or emphasize the target sounds: /ks/. Guide children to determine if the /ks/ sounds are at the beginning of the word or at the end. Have children write the letter *x* in the corresponding box (first box if /ks/ is at the beginning, last box if /ks/ is at the end). Children should notice that the letter *x* appears only at the end of these words.

Sound Boxes

Name: _____ Date: _____

Consonant Qq (qu)

1.

2.

3.

4.

To the teacher: Say each picture name and have children repeat. Stretch or emphasize the target sounds: /kw/. Guide children to determine if the /kw/ sounds are at the beginning of the word or at the end. Have children write the letters *qu* in the corresponding box (first box if /kw/ is at the beginning, last box if /kw/ is at the end). Children should notice that the letters *qu* appear only at the beginnings of these words.

Sound Boxes

Name: _____ Date: _____

Short a

1.

2.

3.

4.

5.

To the teacher: Each box represents one sound and its corresponding spelling. Say each picture name and have children repeat. Guide children to count each sound in the word. Children can tap, chop, hold up one finger for each sound, or mark each box with a counter. Then have children write the letter or letters for each sound in the boxes.

Sound Boxes

Name: _____   Date: _____

Short *i*

1.

2.

3.

4.

5.

To the teacher: Each box represents one sound and its corresponding spelling. Say each picture name and have children repeat. Guide children to count each sound in the word. Children can tap, chop, hold up one finger for each sound, or mark each box with a counter. Then have children write the letter or letters for each sound in the boxes. Note: The digraph *ch* is one sound, so write *ch* in one box.

Sound Boxes

Name: _____ Date: _____

Short o

1.

2.

3.

4.

5.

To the teacher: Each box represents one sound and its corresponding spelling. Say each picture name and have children repeat. Guide children to count each sound in the word. Children can tap, chop, hold up one finger for each sound, or mark each box with a counter. Then have children write the letter or letters for each sound in the boxes. Note: The spelling *ck* is one sound, so write *ck* in one box.

The Megabook of Spelling: Grades K–2 © Wiley Blevins, Scholastic Inc.

Sound Boxes

Name: _____   Date: _____

Short *u*

1.
2.
3.
4.
5.

To the teacher: Each box represents one sound and its corresponding spelling. Say each picture name and have children Repeat. Guide children to count each sound in the word. Children can tap, chop, hold up one finger for each sound, or mark each box with a counter. Then have children write the letter or letters for each sound in the boxes.

Sound Boxes

Name: _____   Date: _____

Short e

1.
2.
3.
4.
5.

To the teacher: Each box represents one sound and its corresponding spelling. Say each picture name and have children repeat. Guide children to count each sound in the word. Children can tap, chop, hold up one finger for each sound, or mark each box with a counter. Then have children write the letter or letters for each sound in the boxes.

The Megabook of Spelling: Grades K–2 © Wiley Blevins, Scholastic Inc.

Sound Boxes

Consonant Blends (l-blends)

1.
2.
3.
4.
5.

To the teacher: Each box represents one sound and its corresponding spelling. Say each picture name and have children repeat. Guide children to count each sound in the word. Children can tap, chop, hold up one finger for each sound, or mark each box with a counter. Then have children write the letter or letters for each sound in the boxes. Note: The spelling *ck* is one sound, so write *ck* in one box.

Sound Boxes

Name: _____   Date: _____

Consonant Blends (s-blends)

1.
2.
3.
4.
5.

To the teacher: Each box represents one sound and its corresponding spelling. Say each picture name and have children repeat. Guide children to count each sound in the word. Children can tap, chop, hold up one finger for each sound, or mark each box with a counter. Then have children write the letter or letters for each sound in the boxes. Note: The spelling *ll* is one sound, so write *ll* in one box. Also, it is difficult to separate the *n* and *k*. So, it's easier to place the spelling *nk* in one box.

The Megabook of Spelling: Grades K–2 © Wiley Blevins, Scholastic Inc.

Sound Boxes

Name: _____ Date: _____

Consonant Blends (*r*-blends)

1.
2.
3.
4.
5.

To the teacher: Each box represents one sound and its corresponding spelling. Say each picture name and have children repeat. Guide children to count each sound in the word. Children can tap, chop, hold up one finger for each sound, or mark each box with a counter. Then have children write the letter or letters for each sound in the boxes. Note: The spellings *ss* and *ea* each represents one sound, so write *ss* or *ea* in one box.

36   The Megabook of Spelling: Grades K–2 © Wiley Blevins, Scholastic Inc.

Sound Boxes

Name: _____ Date: _____

Digraph *sh*

1.
2.
3.
4.
5.

To the teacher: Each box represents one sound and its corresponding spelling. Say each picture name and have children repeat. Guide children to count each sound in the word. Children can tap, chop, hold up one finger for each sound, or mark each box with a counter. Then have children write the letter or letters for each sound in the boxes. Note: The digraph *sh* is one sound, so write *sh* in one box.

The Megabook of Spelling: Grades K–2 © Wiley Blevins, Scholastic Inc.

Sound Boxes

Digraph *th*

Name: _____   Date: _____

1.
2.
3.
4.
5.

To the teacher: Each box represents one sound and its corresponding spelling. Say each picture name and have children repeat. Guide children to count each sound in the word. Children can tap, chop, hold up one finger for each sound, or mark each box with a counter. Then have children write the letter or letters for each sound in the boxes. Note: The digraph *th* is one sound, so write *th* in one box.

Sound Boxes

Name: _____ Date: _____

Digraph *ch*, Trigraph *tch*

1.
2.
3.
4.
5.

To the teacher: Each box represents one sound and its corresponding spelling. Say each picture name and have children repeat. Guide children to count each sound in the word. Children can tap, chop, hold up one finger for each sound, or mark each box with a counter. Then have children write the letter or letters for each sound in the boxes. Note: The digraph *ch* and trigraph *tch* both have one sound, so write *ch* or *tch* in one box.

The Megabook of Spelling: Grades K–2 © Wiley Blevins, Scholastic Inc.

Sound Boxes

Name: _____ Date: _____

Digraph wh
Complete the Sentence

Write the word to finish each sentence.

> When   Where   Why   Which   white

1. _____ will the game start?

2. _____ pet is the best to get?

3. _____ are you sad?

4. _____ is my lost book?

5. My dog is black and _____.

To the teacher: The "wh" words are mostly question words that children need to learn to read and spell early on. It is best to use them in context sentences. Some words contain less common or irregular spellings, such as *where* and *who*.

Sound Boxes

Name: _____ Date: _____

Digraph *ng*, Blend *nk*

1.
2.
3.
4.
5.

To the teacher: Say each picture name and have children repeat. Guide children to count each sound in the word. Children can tap, chop, hold up one finger for each sound, or mark each box with a counter. Then have children write the letter or letters for each sound in the boxes. Note: It is difficult to separate the *n* and *g* or *k*. So, it's easier to place the spellings *ng* or *nk* in one box.

Sound Boxes

Name: _____ Date: _____

Final e

1.
2.
3.
4.
5.

To the teacher: Say each picture name and have children repeat. Guide children to count each sound in the word. Children can tap, chop, hold up one finger for each sound, or mark each box with a counter. Then have children write the letter or letters for each sound in the boxes. Note: The gray box stands for the final, silent *e*.

Sound Boxes

Name: _____   Date: _____

Long a

1.
2.
3.
3.
5.

To the teacher: Each box represents one sound and its corresponding spelling. Say each picture name and have children repeat. Guide children to count each sound in the word. Children can tap, chop, hold up one finger for each sound, or mark each box with a counter. Then have children write the letter or letters for each sound in the boxes.

The Megabook of Spelling: Grades K–2 © Wiley Blevins, Scholastic Inc.

Sound Boxes

Name: _____ Date: _____

Long e

1.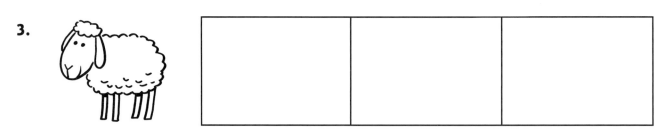

2.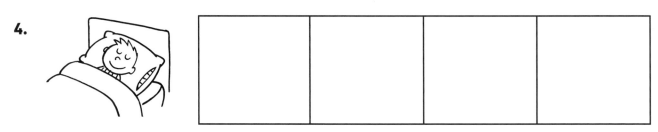

3.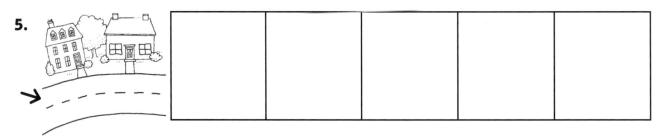

4.

5.

To the teacher: Each box represents one sound and its corresponding spelling. Say each picture name and have children repeat. Guide children to count each sound in the word. Children can tap, chop, hold up one finger for each sound, or mark each box with a counter. Then have children write the letter or letters for each sound in the boxes.

Sound Boxes

Name: _____   Date: _____

Long o

1.
2.
3.
4.
5.

To the teacher: Each box represents one sound and its corresponding spelling. Say each picture name and have children repeat. Guide children to count each sound in the word. Children can tap, chop, hold up one finger for each sound, or mark each box with a counter. Then have children write the letter or letters for each sound in the boxes.

The Megabook of Spelling: Grades K–2 © Wiley Blevins, Scholastic Inc.

Sound Boxes

Name: _____ Date: _____

Long *i*

1.
2.
3.
4.
5.

To the teacher: Each box represents one sound and its corresponding spelling. Say each picture name and have children repeat. Guide children to count each sound in the word. Children can tap, chop, hold up one finger for each sound, or mark each box with a counter. Then have children write the letter or letters for each sound in the boxes.

Sound Boxes

Name: _____ Date: _____

Long u

1.

2.

3.

4.

5. Teacher's Choice!

To the teacher: Say each picture name and have children repeat. Guide children to count each sound in the word. Children can tap, chop, hold up one finger for each sound, or mark each box with a counter. Then have children write the letter or letters for each sound in the boxes. Note: The gray box stands for the final, silent *e*.

The Megabook of Spelling: Grades K–2 © Wiley Blevins, Scholastic Inc.

47

Sound Boxes

Name: _____ Date: _____

r-Controlled Vowels er, ir, ur

1.

2.

3.

4.

5.

To the teacher: Each box represents one sound and its corresponding spelling. It is difficult to separate r-controlled vowel spellings, which is why they are often referred to as "glued" sounds. So, it's easier to place the spelling in one box. Say each picture name and have children repeat. Guide children to count each sound in the word. Children can tap, chop, hold up one finger for each sound, or mark each box with a counter. Then have children write the letter or letters for each sound in the boxes.

48 The Megabook of Spelling: Grades K–2 © Wiley Blevins, Scholastic Inc.

Name: _____   Date: _____

Sound Boxes

r-Controlled Vowel ar

1.
2.
3.
4.
5.

To the teacher: Each box represents one sound and its corresponding spelling. It is difficult to separate r-controlled vowel spellings, which is why they are often referred to as "glued" sounds. So, it's easier to place the spelling in one box. Say each picture name and have children repeat. Guide children to count each sound in the word. Children can tap, chop, hold up one finger for each sound, or mark each box with a counter. Then have children write the letter or letters for each sound in the boxes.

The Megabook of Spelling: Grades K–2 © Wiley Blevins, Scholastic Inc.

Sound Boxes

Name: _____ Date: _____

r-Controlled Vowels
or, ore, oor, our

1.
2.
3.
4.
5.

To the teacher: It is difficult to separate *r*-controlled vowel spellings, which is why they are often referred to as "glued" sounds. So, it's easier to place the spelling in one box. Note: The gray box stands for the final, silent *e*.

Sound Boxes

Name: _____ Date: _____

r-Controlled Vowels
air, ear, are

1.

2.

3.

4.

5.

To the teacher: It is difficult to separate *r*-controlled vowel spellings, which is why they are often referred to as "glued" sounds. So, it's easier to place the spelling in one box.

The Megabook of Spelling: Grades K–2 © Wiley Blevins, Scholastic Inc.

Sound Boxes

Name: _____ Date: _____

Diphthongs oi, oy

1.

2.

3.

4.

5.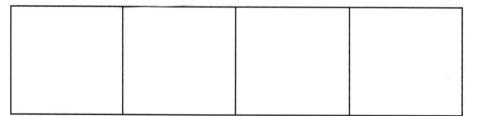

To the teacher: Each box represents one sound and its corresponding spelling. Say each picture name and have children repeat. Guide children to count each sound in the word. Children can tap, chop, hold up one finger for each sound, or mark each box with a counter. Then have children write the letter or letters for each sound in the boxes.

Name: _____ Date: _____

Diphthongs *ou, ow*

1. [house picture] | | | | (gray box)

2. [shouting boy picture] | | | |

3. [town picture] | | | |

4. [down arrow picture] | | | |

5. [clown picture] | | | |

To the teacher: Each box represents one sound and its corresponding spelling. Say each picture name and have children repeat. Guide children to count each sound in the word. Children can tap, chop, hold up one finger for each sound, or mark each box with a counter. Then have children write the letter or letters for each sound in the boxes. Note: The gray box stands for the final, silent *e*.

The Megabook of Spelling: Grades K–2 © Wiley Blevins, Scholastic Inc.

Sound Boxes

Name: _____ Date: _____

Complex Vowel /ô/ a(l), au, aw

1.
2.
3.
4.
5.

To the teacher: Each box represents one sound and its corresponding spelling. Say each picture name and have children repeat. Guide children to count each sound in the word. Children can tap, chop, hold up one finger for each sound, or mark each box with a counter. Then have children write the letter or letters for each sound in the boxes.

Sound Boxes

Name: _____ Date: _____

Short oo

To the teacher: Each box represents one sound and its corresponding spelling. Say each picture name and have children repeat. Guide children to count each sound in the word. Children can tap, chop, hold up one finger for each sound, or mark each box with a counter. Then have children write the letter or letters for each sound in the boxes.

Sound Boxes

Name: _____ Date: _____

Long oo (oo, ew, ue, oe)

1.
2.
3.
4.
5.

To the teacher: Each box represents one sound and its corresponding spelling. Say each picture name and have children repeat. Guide children to count each sound in the word. Children can tap, chop, hold up one finger for each sound, or mark each box with a counter. Then have children write the letter or letters for each sound in the boxes.

Sound Boxes

Name: _____   Date: _____

Silent Letters

1.
2.
3.
4.
5.

To the teacher: Each box represents one sound and its corresponding spelling. Say each picture name and have children repeat. Guide children to count each sound in the word. Children can tap, chop, hold up one finger for each sound, or mark each box with a counter. Then have children write the letter or letters for each sound in the boxes. Note: The gray box stands for the final, silent *e*.

The Megabook of Spelling: Grades K–2 © Wiley Blevins, Scholastic Inc.

Syllable Boxes

Name: _____ Date: _____

Prefixes un-, re-

1.

2.

3.

4.

5.

To the teacher: Each box represents one **syllable** and its corresponding spelling. Say each picture name and have children repeat. Guide children to count each syllable in the word. Children can clap or count their chin drops. Then have children write the letters for each syllable in the boxes. It is important that the prefix be in a box by itself.

Name: _____ Date: _____

Suffix -ing

1.

2.

3.

4.

5.

To the teacher: Each box represents one **syllable** and its corresponding spelling. Say each picture name and have children repeat. Guide students to count each syllable in the word. Children can clap or count their chin drops. Then, have children write the letters for each syllable in the boxes. It is important that the suffix be in a box by itself.

The Megabook of Spelling: Grades K–2 © Wiley Blevins, Scholastic Inc.

Syllable Boxes

Name: _____ Date: _____

Suffix -ed

1.

2.

3.

4.

5.

To the teacher: Each box represents one **syllable** and its corresponding spelling. Say each picture name and have children repeat. Guide children to count each syllable in the word. Children can clap or count their chin drops. Then have children write the letters for each syllable in the boxes. It is important that the suffix be in a box by itself.

Syllable Boxes

Name: _____   Date: _____

Suffixes -ful, -less

1.

2.

3.

4.

5.

To the teacher: Each box represents one **syllable** and its corresponding spelling. Say each picture name and have children repeat. Guide children to count each syllable in the word. Children can clap or count their chin drops. Then have children write the letters for each syllable in the boxes. It is important that the suffix be in a box by itself.

Syllable Boxes

Name: _____ Date: _____

Suffixes -y, -ly

1.

2.

3.

4.

5.

To the teacher: Each box represents one **syllable** and its corresponding spelling. Say each picture name and have children repeat. Guide children to count each syllable in the word. Children can clap or count their chin drops. Then have children write the letters for each syllable in the boxes. It is important that the suffix be in a box by itself.

Syllable Boxes

Name: _____ Date: _____

Final Stable Syllables
(tion, sion, ture, sure)

1.

2.

3.

4.

5.

To the teacher: Each box represents one **syllable** and its corresponding spelling. Say each picture name and have children repeat. Guide children to count each syllable in the word. Children can clap or count their chin drops. Then have children write the letters for each syllable in the boxes. It is important that the suffix be in a box by itself.

The Megabook of Spelling: Grades K–2 © Wiley Blevins, Scholastic Inc.

Syllable Boxes

Name: _____ Date: _____

Compound Words

1.

2.

3.

4.

5.

To the teacher: Each box represents one **syllable** and its corresponding spelling. Say each picture name and have children repeat. Guide children to count each syllable in the word. Children can clap or count their chin drops. Then have children write the letters for each syllable in the boxes.

Syllable Boxes

Name: _____   Date: _____

Compound Words

1.

2.

3.

4.

5.

To the teacher: Each box represents one **syllable** and its corresponding spelling. Say each picture name and have children repeat. Guide children to count each syllable in the word. Children can clap or count their chin drops. Then have children write the letters for each syllable in the boxes.

Syllable Boxes

Name: _____ Date: _____

Closed Syllables

1.

2.

3.

4.

5.

To the teacher: Each box represents one **syllable** and its corresponding spelling. Say each picture name and have children repeat. Guide children to count each syllable in the word. Children can clap or count their chin drops. Then have children write the letters for each syllable in the boxes.

Name: _____   Date: _____

Closed Syllables

1.
2.
3.
4.
5.

To the teacher: Each box represents one **syllable** and its corresponding spelling. Say each picture name, and have children repeat. Guide children to count each syllable in the word. Children can clap or count their chin drops. Then have children write the letters for each syllable in the boxes.

Syllable Boxes

Name: _____   Date: _____

Open Syllables

1.

2.

3.

4.

5.

To the teacher: Each box represents one **syllable** and its corresponding spelling. Say each picture name and have children repeat. Guide children to count each syllable in the word. Children can clap or count their chin drops. Then have children write the letters for each syllable in the boxes.

Name: _____ Date: _____

Syllable Boxes

Open Syllables

1.
2.
3.
4.
5.

To the teacher: Each box represents one **syllable** and its corresponding spelling. Say each picture name and have children repeat. Guide children to count each syllable in the word. Children can clap or count their chin drops. Then have children write the letters for each syllable in the boxes.

The Megabook of Spelling: Grades K–2 © Wiley Blevins, Scholastic Inc.

Syllable Boxes

Name: _____ Date: _____

r-Controlled Vowel Syllables

1.

2.

3.

4.

5.

To the teacher: Each box represents one **syllable** and its corresponding spelling. Say each picture name and have children repeat. Guide children to count each syllable in the word. Children can clap or count their chin drops. Then have children write the letters for each syllable in the boxes.

Name: _____   Date: _____

r-Controlled Vowel Syllables

1.
2.
3.
4.
5.

To the teacher: Each box represents one **syllable** and its corresponding spelling. Say each picture name and have children repeat. Guide children to count each syllable in the word. Children can clap or count their chin drops. Then have children write the letters for each syllable in the boxes.

The Megabook of Spelling: Grades K–2 © Wiley Blevins, Scholastic Inc.

Syllable Boxes

Name: _____ Date: _____

Vowel Team Syllables

1.
2.
3.
4.
5.

To the teacher: Each box represents one **syllable** and its corresponding spelling. Say each picture name and have children repeat. Guide children to count each syllable in the word. Children can clap or count their chin drops. Then have children write the letters for each syllable in the boxes.

Syllable Boxes

Name: _____   Date: _____

Vowel Team Syllables

1.
2.
3.
4.
5.

To the teacher: Each box represents one **syllable** and its corresponding spelling. Say each picture name and have children repeat. Guide children to count each syllable in the word. Children can clap or count their chin drops. Then have children write the letters for each syllable in the boxes.

The Megabook of Spelling: Grades K–2 © Wiley Blevins, Scholastic Inc.

Syllable Boxes

Name: _____ Date: _____

Consonant + *le* Syllables

1.
2.
3.
4.
5.

To the teacher: Each box represents one **syllable** and its corresponding spelling. Say each picture name and have children repeat. Guide children to count each syllable in the word. Children can clap or count their chin drops. Then have children write the letters for each syllable in the boxes.

Syllable Boxes

Name: _____ Date: _____

Consonant + *le* Syllables

1.
2.
3.
4.
5.

To the teacher: Each box represents one **syllable** and its corresponding spelling. Say each picture name and have children repeat. Guide children to count each syllable in the word. Children can clap or count their chin drops. Then have children write the letters for each syllable in the boxes.

Syllable Boxes

Name: _____   Date: _____

Final-e Syllables

1.

2.

3.

4.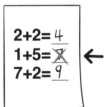

5.

To the teacher: Each box represents one **syllable** and its corresponding spelling. Say each picture name and have children repeat. Guide children to count each syllable in the word. Children can clap or count their chin drops. Then have children write the letters for each syllable in the boxes.

76   The Megabook of Spelling: Grades K–2 © Wiley Blevins, Scholastic Inc.

Name: _____   Date: _____

Syllable Boxes

Final-e Syllables

1.
2.
3.
4.
5.

To the teacher: Each box represents one **syllable** and its corresponding spelling. Say each picture name and have children repeat. Guide children to count each syllable in the word. Children can clap or count their chin drops. Then have children write the letters for each syllable in the boxes.

The Megabook of Spelling: Grades K–2 © Wiley Blevins, Scholastic Inc.

Principle 4: Daily Spelling and Writing Activities

Skills Practiced

Phonemic Awareness

Handwriting

Spelling

Decoding

Dictation

Writing

Section 2 downloadables are available here.

SECTION 2

Dictation

Children should engage in encoding (spelling/writing) activities every day and in every phonics lesson. It takes longer to transfer these phonics patterns to writing than reading. These activities can vary, each with an important instructional focus. They include:

- **dictation** — guided spelling of letters, words, and simple sentences
- **word building** — using letter cards or magnetic letters to manipulate sounds and spellings in a series of words
- **word sorts** — with discussions about key spelling observations that can aid in writing
- **writing about decodable texts** — an application of skills activity that also checks comprehension.

Extra attention must also be afforded to the irregular high-frequency words (e.g., *said, was, they*) that many children struggle with spelling because of their irregular or less-common spelling patterns.

Materials Needed	The following pages provide guided practice in dictation. • Pages 81–90 provide instruction and templates for four levels of dictation. • Pages 91–97 provide differentiated dictation word sets. **Optional:** sound (Elkonin) boxes • counters • alphabet wall chart • sound-spelling cards • high-frequency words chart
Length of Activity	5–10 minutes
Location	school or home

Dictation Routine

Use the following routine for dictation.

Routine Steps	Sample Teacher Talk
Step 1: Dictate the Word (or Sound) State aloud the first word in the dictation line and have children repeat it. For those who have difficulty hearing the sounds in the words, you can provide three levels of support. • **Level 1:** Say the sounds more slowly while moving your hands from right to left while facing the class to illustrate beginning, middle, and end. • **Level 2:** Model the blending for each sound in the word. In effect, you help children hear and write one sound at a time. • **Level 3:** Have children segment the word using sound (Elkonin) boxes and counters, and then replace each counter with a letter or spelling. Then, have children write the word. (Use the Tap, Spell, Write templates on pages 88–90.) **Note:** For kindergarten (and early Grade 1), you will start by saying a sound, then asking children to write the letter or spelling to build handwriting fluency. This is a great opportunity to model letter formation correction (as needed) and articulation to help children distinguish similar sounds.	*I want you to write a word that can be sounded out. The word is* **sat**. *Say* **sat**. [The children chorally say *sat*.] *Sound* **sat**. [Slowly say the sounds in *sat* without any break and show beginning, middle, and end with right to left hand motions.] Then, move your hand back to the beginning position and ask: *What's the beginning sound?* (/sss/) *Write /sss/.* [Wait for children to finish.] *What word are you writing?* (sat) *The beginning sound was...?* (/sss/) *Next sound?* (/aaa/) *Write /aaa/.* [Wait for children to finish.] *What word are you writing?* (sat) *What do you have so far?* (/sssaaa/) *Last sound?* (/t/) *Write /t/.* When children finish, ask them to chorally tell you the sounds in *sat* as you write the word on the board. **Note:** For children using sound boxes and counters, guide them to replace each counter with a letter or spelling.

Section 2

Dictation

Routine Steps (continued)	Sample Teacher Talk (continued)
Step 2: Provide Feedback Walk around and give help as necessary. • This may include showing children the correct stroke procedure for writing letters or directing them to the correct spelling on the alphabet wall chart or sound-spelling card. • In the case of multiple spellings for a single sound (such as *c*, *k*, and *ck*), tell children which spelling is correct and briefly explain why. For example, the *ck* spelling for /k/ appears at the end of a word and is preceded by a short vowel sound (e.g., *sick*, *back*, *rock*, *luck*, *deck*). These on-the-spot reminders of rules and generalizations in English spelling are important differentiated additions. (See Section 13 for more details.) Continue this procedure for each word in the dictation line.	[Offer corrective feedback.]
Step 3: Children Self-Correct As each word is completed, provide feedback by writing the answer on the board so that children can correct their work. A key component of dictation is self-correction, in which children begin to notice and correct their errors. This can also aid in continuing the conversation about English spellings.	[Write answers on the board for self-correction.]
Step 4: Dictate Sentences For the dictation sentence, read the entire sentence aloud and then focus on one word or phrase at a time. For multisyllabic words, do one syllable at a time. While children are writing, walk around and monitor their work, paying more attention to those who are likely to experience difficulty. **Note:** This teacher-assisted sound-by-sound process is critical for children who cannot segment sounds. Don't take shortcuts by just giving children the word, waiting for them to finish, and then writing the answer on the board. Some children will wait and copy what is on the board and will not learn to become independent. This is their time to try, to explore, to make their best attempts.	Say: *Now, you will write a sentence with three words. The sentence is:* **Sam is sad.** *Repeat it.* (Sam is sad.) *What is the first word?* (Sam) *How do we start a sentence?* (With a capital letter) *Is* **Sam** *a word we can sound out or a word on our high-frequency chart? Sound* **Sam**. [Use hand motions as before.] *First sound?* [Pause for children to say the first sound.] *Write it. What word are you writing? What do you have so far? Next sound?* [Pause for children to respond.] *Write it.* [Continue in a similar manner until the word is done.] *What sentence are you writing?* (Sam is sad.) *What have you written so far?* (Sam) *What is the next word?* (is) *If you know how to spell it, go ahead and write it. If you are not sure, check the high-frequency chart.* Continue this procedure with *sad*, treating it as a word that can be sounded out.

TEMPLATE #1 (Use with kindergarten and Grade 1.)

Dictation: Sounds and Words

Dictation: Sounds and Words

Name: _____ Date: _____

Sounds and Letters

1. _____   2. _____

3. _____   4. _____

Words

1st Attempt   2nd Attempt

5. _____   _____

6. _____   _____

7. _____   _____

8. _____   _____

The Megabook of Spelling: Grades K–2 © Wiley Blevins, Scholastic Inc.

To the teacher: See page 91 for the lists of sounds and words for dictation. Dictate each sound first. Have children repeat, then write the letter for the sound. Continue with the words. Have children write each word in the 1st Attempt column. The first two words contain the target phonics skill. The second two words are your choice. It is great to contrast the new vowel sound with previously taught vowel sound-spellings. They can be additional words with the target skill or words with review skills with which children need additional practice. Write the answers on the board, then have children write the word a second time, correcting any mistakes in the 2nd Attempt column. You can extend the activity by having children write a dictated sentence on the back of the paper.

Dictation: Sounds and Words

Name: _____ Date: _____

Sounds and Letters

1. _____ 2. _____

3. _____ 4. _____

Words

| 1st Attempt | 2nd Attempt |

5. _____ _____

6. _____ _____

7. _____ _____

8. _____ _____

TEMPLATE #2 (Use with Grades 1 and 2.)

Dictation: Sound-Spellings

Dictation: Sound-Spellings

Name: _____ Date: _____

Sounds and Letters

1. _____ _____ _____ _____

Words and Sentence

        1st Attempt   2nd Attempt

2. _____ _____

3. _____ _____

4. _____ _____

5. _____ _____

6. _____ _____

_____

To the teacher: See pages 92–94 for the lists of sound-spellings, words, and sentences for dictation. Dictate each sound-spelling first. Have children repeat, then write the letter, letters, or multiple spellings for the sound (one spelling per blank). Continue with the words. Have children write each word in the 1st Attempt column. The first two words contain the target phonics skill. The second two words are your choice. They can be additional words with the target skill or words with review skills with which children need additional practice. Write the answers on the board, then have children write the word a second time, correcting any mistakes in the 2nd Attempt column. For the sentence, say the sentence and guide children to count the number of words. Then guide them to write one word or phrase at a time. Keep repeating the sentence in meaningful phrase chunks for children who need the support.

Dictation: Sound-Spellings

Name: _____   Date: _____

Sounds and Letters

1. _____ _____ _____ _____

Words and Sentence

1st Attempt   2nd Attempt

2. _____   _____

3. _____   _____

4. _____   _____

5. _____   _____

6. _____

_____

TEMPLATE #3 (Use with Grade 2.)

Dictation: Word Pyramids

Dictation: Word Pyramids

Name: _____ Date: _____

Word Pyramids

1.   2.

_____   _____

_____   _____

_____   _____

_____   _____

3.   4.

_____   _____

_____   _____

_____   _____

_____   _____

To the teacher: See pages 95–97 for the lists of words for dictation. Dictate each word. Have children repeat, then have them write the word on the first or next available line. Write the answers on the board, then have children self-correct. Discuss any spelling changes or other features (e.g., change *y* to *i*; a prefix is its own syllable; spell one syllable at a time; notice the parts of the word that are maintained across the related word set). These word chains provide differentiation for a wide range of student needs while leveling up the spelling work for children below grade-level expectations.

Dictation: Word Pyramids

Name: _____ Date: _____

Word Pyramids

1.

_____

_____

_____

2.

_____

_____

_____

3.

_____

_____

_____

4.

_____

_____

_____

TEMPLATE #4

Dictation: Tap, Spell, Write

Section 2
Dictation

Dictation

Name: _____ Date: _____

Tap, Spell, Write (I)

1.
2.
3.
4.
5.

88 — *The Megabook of Spelling: Grades K–2* © Wiley Blevins, Scholastic Inc.

To the teacher: There are three versions of this template for words with three to five sounds. You can use your own list of words for dictation or see pages 111–118. Have children tap (count) the sounds in the word and mark a dot (or place a counter) on each box for each sound. Then, have them write the letter or letters for each sound in the corresponding box. Next, have them write the word again on the lines in their best handwriting. Finally, have them read the completed word list.

Dictation

Name: _____ Date: _____

Tap, Spell, Write (I)

1.

2.

3.

4.

5.

Dictation

Name: _____ Date: _____

Tap, Spell, Write (2)

1.
2.
3.
4.
5.

Dictation

Name: _____   Date: _____

Tap, Spell, Write (3)

1.

2.

3.

4.

5.

Kindergarten – Grade 1 (Use with Template #1.)

Consonants and Short Vowels

(*NOTE: Modify the sounds and words based on your program's phonics scope and sequence.)*

Short *a*
1. /a/
2. /s/
3. /m/
4. /t/
5. sat
6. mat
7. (Teacher's choice: Review words and/or high-frequency words.)
8. (Teacher's choice: Review words and/or high-frequency words.)

Short *i*
1. /i/
2. /a/
3. /b/
4. /d/
5. bit
6. fit
7. (Teacher's choice: Review words and/or high-frequency words.)
8. (Teacher's choice: Review words and/or high-frequency words.)

*Note: Review words could be *bat* and *fat* to contrast short *i* and short *a*.

Short *o*
1. /o/
2. /a/
3. /p/
4. /h/
5. hop
6. hot
7. (Teacher's choice: Review words and/or high-frequency words.)
8. (Teacher's choice: Review words and/or high-frequency words.)

Short *u*
1. /u/
2. /o/
3. /g/
4. /j/
5. run
6. rug
7. (Teacher's choice: Review words and/or high-frequency words.)
8. (Teacher's choice: Review words and/or high-frequency words.)

Short *e*
1. /e/
2. /u/
3. /w/
4. /l/
5. wet
6. well
7. (Teacher's choice: Review words and/or high-frequency words.)
8. (Teacher's choice: Review words and/or high-frequency words.)

Section 2
Dictation

Section 2
Dictation

Grade 1 – Grade 2 (Use with Template #2.)

Advanced Phonics Concepts

Consonant Blends (*l*-blends)
1. sl fl bl pl
2. *flag*
3. *plot*
4. (Teacher's choice: Review words and/or high-frequency words.)
5. (Teacher's choice: Review words and/or high-frequency words.)
6. Do not slip with a glass in your hand.

Consonant Blends (*s*-blends)
1. st sm sn sw
2. *spell*
3. *stops*
4. (Teacher's choice: Review words and/or high-frequency words.)
5. (Teacher's choice: Review words and/or high-frequency words.)
6. I smell a good snack at that spot.

Consonant Blends (*r*-blends)
1. br dr tr gr
2. *crab*
3. *frog*
4. (Teacher's choice: Review words and/or high-frequency words.)
5. (Teacher's choice: Review words and/or high-frequency words.)
6. Did you rip your dress on the trip?

Digraph *sh*
1. sh s h st
2. *ship*
3. *smash*
4. (Teacher's choice: Review words and/or high-frequency words.)
5. (Teacher's choice: Review words and/or high-frequency words.)
6. Rush in the shop and get some fresh fish.

Digraph *th*
1. th th (voiced) sh tr
2. *thin*
3. *that*
4. (Teacher's choice: Review words and/or high-frequency words.)
5. (Teacher's choice: Review words and/or high-frequency words.)
6. This is a very thick bathmat.

Digraph *ch* and Trigraph *tch*
1. ch tch sh th
2. *chop*
3. *patch*
4. (Teacher's choice: Review words and/or high-frequency words.)
5. (Teacher's choice: Review words and/or high-frequency words.)
6. I had chips for lunch.

Digraph *wh*
1. wh ch sh th
2. *when*
3. *which*
4. (Teacher's choice: Review words and/or high-frequency words.)
5. (Teacher's choice: Review words and/or high-frequency words.)
6. Which wig will you get?

Digraph *ng* and Blend *nk*
1. ng nk nt nd
2. *bring*
3. *drink*
4. (Teacher's choice: Review words and/or high-frequency words.)
5. (Teacher's choice: Review words and/or high-frequency words.)
6. The king likes to think of sad songs.

Section 2
Dictation

Final e
1. a   a_e   i   i_e
2. brave
3. slide
4. (Teacher's choice: Review words and/or high-frequency words.)
5. (Teacher's choice: Review words and/or high-frequency words.)
6. Hope will hop on the bus and ride it home.

Long a
1. a   ai   ay   a_e
2. train
3. stay
4. (Teacher's choice: Review words and/or high-frequency words.)
5. (Teacher's choice: Review words and/or high-frequency words.)
6. Can Jane and Dave play in the rain in May?

Long e
1. e   ea   ee   y
2. sleep
3. team
4. (Teacher's choice: Review words and/or high-frequency words.)
5. (Teacher's choice: Review words and/or high-frequency words.)
6. Did we dream of fluffy sheep jumping in a tree?

Long o
1. o   oa   ow   oe
2. float
3. show
4. (Teacher's choice: Review words and/or high-frequency words.)
5. (Teacher's choice: Review words and/or high-frequency words.)
6. He puts on a thick coat when he goes to play in the snow.

Long i
1. i   igh   y   ie
2. bright
3. cry
4. (Teacher's choice: Review words and/or high-frequency words.)
5. (Teacher's choice: Review words and/or high-frequency words.)
6. I might try to bake a pumpkin pie.

Long u
1. u   u_e   ew   ue
2. cute
3. unit
4. (Teacher's choice: Review words and/or high-frequency words.)
5. (Teacher's choice: Review words and/or high-frequency words.)
6. Did she rescue a few dogs?

r-Controlled Vowels er, ir, ur
1. er   ir   ur   r
2. hurt
3. first
4. (Teacher's choice: Review words and/or high-frequency words.)
5. (Teacher's choice: Review words and/or high-frequency words.)
6. Her purple shirt is dirty.

r-Controlled Vowel ar
1. ar   er   ir   ur
2. farm
3. start
4. (Teacher's choice: Review words and/or high-frequency words.)
5. (Teacher's choice: Review words and/or high-frequency words.)
6. Mark has a little barn in his yard.

Note: When dictating words for long and complex vowels, it is often helpful to focus each day's dictation on only one or two patterns to emphasize them. For example, dictate words with -ird, -irt, -irth on one day to emphasize that the *ir* spelling is often used when the next sound is /d/, /t/, or /th/. This helps build children's statistical awareness of spelling patterns.

Section 2

Dictation

r-Controlled Vowels *or, ore, oar, oor, our*
1. or   ore   ar   er
2. fork
3. shore
4. (Teacher's choice: Review words and/or high-frequency words.)
5. (Teacher's choice: Review words and/or high-frequency words.)
6. I used four old boards to make the door for my fort.

r-Controlled Vowels *air, ear, ere, are*
1. air   ear   ere   are
2. there (direction)
3. pear (fruit)
4. (Teacher's choice: Review words and/or high-frequency words.)
5. (Teacher's choice: Review words and/or high-frequency words.)
6. Would you share your chair with a big bear?

Diphthong *oi/oy*
1. oi   oy   oa   ow
2. soil
3. toy
4. (Teacher's choice: Review words and/or high-frequency words.)
5. (Teacher's choice: Review words and/or high-frequency words.)
6. Did the boy join Roy's team?

Diphthong *ou/ow*
1. ou   ow   oi   oy
2. brown
3. ground
4. (Teacher's choice: Review words and/or high-frequency words.)
5. (Teacher's choice: Review words and/or high-frequency words.)
6. I found a new house in town.

Complex Vowel /ô/ *a, au, aw*
1. au   aw   all   ou
2. straw
3. sauce
4. (Teacher's choice: Review words and/or high-frequency words.)
5. (Teacher's choice: Review words and/or high-frequency words.)
6. Paul can draw a small kitten with a black paw.

Short *oo*
1. oo   o   ou   oi
2. good
3. shook
4. (Teacher's choice: Review words and/or high-frequency words.)
5. (Teacher's choice: Review words and/or high-frequency words.)
6. Look at the book I just read!

Long *oo* (*oo, ew, ue, u_e*)
1. oo   ew   ue   u_e
2. glue
3. broom
4. (Teacher's choice: Review words and/or high-frequency words.)
5. (Teacher's choice: Review words and/or high-frequency words.)
6. Is it true that the new moon comes in June?

Silent Letters
1. wr   r   kn   n
2. write
3. know
4. (Teacher's choice: Review words and/or high-frequency words.)
5. (Teacher's choice: Review words and/or high-frequency words.)
6. She knit socks for her friend.

Grade 2 (Use with Template #3.)

Multisyllabic Words

Consonant Blends
(3-letter and complex blends)
1. sing, sting, string, stringing
2. stain, strain, straining, restraining
3. spit, split, splint, splinter
4. scrap, scrape, scraped, scraping

Digraph *sh*
1. hop, shop, ship, hip
2. sell, shell, shells, shellfish
3. rash, trash, trashcan, thrash
4. rush, brush, brushing, brushed

Digraph *th*
1. hat, that, hen, then
2. his, this, these, those
3. thin, think, thick, thickest
4. wit, with, within, without

Digraph *ch* and Trigraph *tch*
1. hat, chat, hip, chip
2. chick, chicken, child, children
3. bun, bunch, bench, punch
4. it, itch, witch, switch

Digraph *wh*
1. hen, when, whenever, whatever
2. whip, whim, whimper, whimpers
3. white, while, whale, whales
4. whisk, whisker, whisper, whispering

Digraph *ng* and Blend *nk*
1. win, wing, swing, sting
2. ring, bring, bringing, stinging
3. tan, tank, thank, thankful
4. sing, sink, stink, think

Final *e*
1. take, taking, retaking, mistaking
2. hop, hope, hopeful, hopefully
3. like, dislike, unlike, unlikable
4. place, placing, replacing, misplacing

Long *a*
1. rain, train, training, retraining
2. play, playing, replaying, replayed
3. paid, repaid, unpaid, underpaid
4. plan, plain, explain, explained

Long *e*
1. read, reading, rereading, misreading
2. steam, stream, downstream, mainstream
3. repeat, retreat, reveal, reappear
4. happy, happily, unhappily, unhappiness

Long *o*
1. cot, coat, raincoat, overcoat
2. fold, unfold, untold, withhold
3. decode, explode, implode, episode
4. know, known, unknown, unknowingly

Long *i*
1. supply, supplies, resupplies, resupplied
2. rely, reply, replied, replying
3. light, sunlight, stoplight, twilight
4. side, inside, roadside, landslide

Long *u*
1. cut, cute, cuter, cutest
2. cub, cube, cubic, cubicle
3. view, review, preview, previewing
4. unit, united, reunited, United States

r*-Controlled Vowels *er, ir, ur
1. skirt, shirt, nightshirt, undershirt
2. serve, reserve, observe, conserve
3. turn, return, returning, returned
4. teacher, leader, baker, driver

r*-Controlled Vowel *ar
1. farm, farmer, farming, farmhouse
2. star, start, starting, restarting
3. large, larger, largest, enlarge
4. mark, remark, remarked, remarkable

Section 2
Dictation

Section 2
Dictation

r-Controlled Vowels *or, ore, oor*
1. door, indoor, outdoor, trapdoor
2. score, scoring, scored, outscored
3. form, perform, misinform, uniform
4. port, export, exported, transported

r-Controlled Vowels *air, ear, ere, are*
1. air, hair, chair, wheelchair
2. compare, prepare, prepared, preparing
3. wear, swear, underwear, outerwear
4. there, therefore, where, wherever

Diphthong *oi/oy*
1. boil, broil, broiling, broiled
2. toy, boy, cowboy, oh boy
3. point, appoint, disappoint, disappointed
4. joy, enjoy, joyful, joyfully

Diphthong *ou/ow*
1. round, ground, background, underground
2. house, doghouse, lighthouse, powerhouse
3. out, without, hangout, cookout
4. down, downtown, sundown, touchdown

Complex Vowel /ô/ *a, au, aw*
1. ball, football, baseball, basketball
2. walk, walking, walked, boardwalk
3. caught, taught, retaught, distraught
4. draw, drawing, withdrawing, withdrawn

Short *oo*
1. hood, fatherhood, likelihood, neighborhood
2. cook, recook, recooked, undercooked
3. book, notebook, handbook, cookbook
4. wood, wooden, driftwood, deadwood

Long *oo* (*oo, ew, u_e*)
1. new, renew, renewed, renewing
2. roof, proof, fireproof, soundproof
3. room, classroom, bathroom, mushroom
4. include, included, including, excluding

Silent Letters
1. wrote, write, rewrite, rewriting
2. know, knowing, known, unknown
3. sign, design, resign, signal
4. comb, climb, crumb, crumble

Prefixes *un-, re-*
1. unfit, unfold, untold, unsold
2. lock, unlock, unlocking, unlocked
3. call, recall, recalling, recalled
4. repay, repaid, retie, retied

Suffix *-ing*
1. landing, handing, standing, planting
2. flashing, mashing, smashing, trashing
3. bake, baking, make, making
4. hop, hopping, stop, stopping

Suffix *-ed*
1. end, ended, landed, melted
2. jog, jogged, slam, slammed
3. save, saved, file, filed
4. picked, biked, thanked, stopped

Suffixes *-ful, -less*
1. care, careless, careful, carefully
2. useful, useless, colorful, colorless
3. hope, hopeless, hopeful, hopefully
4. helpful, helpless, helplessly, helplessness

Suffixes *-y, -ly*
1. jump, jumpy, glass, glassy
2. grassy, itchy, crazy, bouncy
3. calm, calmly, firm, firmly
4. nicely, kindly, certainly, friendly

Compound Words
1. ball, football, baseball, basketball
2. snow, snowfall, snowball, snowman
3. door, doormat, doorbell, doorknob
4. any, anyone, anybody, anything

Section 2
Dictation

Final Stable Syllables
(*tion, sion, ture, sure*)
1. act, action, reject, rejection
2. confuse, confusion, explode, explosion
3. picture, creature, nature, future
4. measure, treasure, pleasure, closure

Closed Syllables
1. napkin, cabin, robin, rabbit
2. mitten, kitten, sudden, puppet
3. plastic, public, publish, pumpkin
4. until, victim, panic, dentist

Open Syllables
1. bacon, baby, basic, bagel
2. lady, lazy, local, locate
3. solo, silo, silent, siren
4. table, cradle, crazy, tidy

***r*-Controlled Vowel Syllables**
1. art, artist, artistic, artful
2. garden, garlic, harvest, harness
3. sister, brother, mother, father
4. thirty, thirsty, thunder, timber

Vowel Team Syllables
1. mailbox, midweek, seaweed, subway
2. enjoy, employ, employing, employed
3. main, remain, remaining, remainder
4. treat, mistreat, mistreated, untreated

Consonant + *le* Syllables
1. little, bottle, brittle, settle
2. table, cable, fable, stable
3. marble, purple, turtle, hurdle
4. able, unable, unstable, enable

Final-*e* Syllables
1. debate, delete, describe, device
2. inside, invade, invite, inflate
3. refine, relate, remote, refuse
4. excite, expose, extreme, excuse

Principle 6: Assessment and Differentiated Supports

Skills Practiced

Phonemic Awareness ☐

Handwriting ☐

Spelling

Decoding ☐

Dictation

Writing ☐

Section 3 downloadables are available here.

SECTION 3

Cumulative Spelling Sentences

Children in any given classroom represent a range of mastery in terms of spelling. Therefore, it is necessary to assess spelling in a cumulative manner, monitor spelling whole class and individually, and provide differentiated support. This makes teaching spelling more challenging and complex for teachers. Simple assessment structures and tools (provided here) and differentiated activities go a long way to better meet all children's spelling needs.

Scoring the Assessments

Use the following guidance to score the cumulative assessments and plan next steps for whole- and small-group instruction.

- Mark the misspelled words.

- Identify any spelling issues and circle them on the "Skills for Additional Support" section at the bottom of the assessment page. This section indicates the skills commonly taught at each grade level.

- Review the "Skills for Additional Support" section for all your students. If a lot of children are not accurately and consistently spelling words with the same skill, add more work with that skill to your whole-class dictation, word building, and word-sort activities. If only a few children are struggling with a specific skill, use this data to form skills-based small groups for targeted instruction and practice.

Materials Needed	The following pages provide guided practice in the cumulative assessment of spelling by using end-of-week dictated sentences. • Pages 99–101 feature templates for cumulative sentence dictation for multiple grades. • Pages 102–107 provide sample cumulative sentences for each phonics skill.
Length of Activity	10 minutes
Location	school or home

Spelling Assessment

Name: _____   Date: _____

Sentences: Kindergarten

1. _____

_____

2. _____

_____

Skills for Additional Support Circle the skills below that the child seems to have issues with.					
Short *a*	Consonants	*m*	*s*	*t*	
Short *i*	Consonants	*p*	*n*	*c*	
Short *o*	Consonants	*f*	*d*	*h*	
Short *e*	Consonants	*r*	*b*	*l*	*k*
Short *u*	Consonants	*g*	*w*	*x*	*v*
Final *e*	Consonants	*j*	*q*	*y*	*z*
Consonant Blends	*l*-Blends	*s*-Blends	*r*-Blends		
Consonant Digraphs	*sh*	*th*	*ch*	*wh*	
OTHER					

The Megabook of Spelling: Grades K–2 © Wiley Blevins, Scholastic Inc.

Spelling Assessment

Name: _____ Date: _____

Sentences: Grade 1

1. _____

_____

_____

2. _____

_____

_____

3. _____

_____

_____

Skills for Additional Support	
Circle the skills below that the child seems to have issues with.	
Short Vowels *a e i o u*	Long Vowels *a e i o u*
l-Blends	*r*-Controlled Vowels *ar er/ir/ur or*
s-Blends	Short and Long *oo*
r-Blends	Diphthongs *ou/ow oi/oy*
Digraphs and Trigraphs *sh th ch/tch wh ng/nk*	Complex Vowel /ô/ *au aw al*
Final *e*	*r*-Controlled Vowels *are/air/ear*
OTHER	

Spelling Assessment

Name: _____ Date: _____

Sentences: Grade 2

1. _____

_____

2. _____

_____

3. _____

_____

4. _____

_____

5. _____

_____

Skills for Additional Support	
Circle the skills below that the child seems to have issues with.	
Short Vowels a e i o u	r-Controlled Vowels ar er/ir/ur or
Long Vowels a e i o u	Short and Long oo
Final e	Diphthongs ou/ow oi/oy
l-Blends, s-Blends, r-Blends	Complex Vowel /ô/ au aw al

Digraphs and Trigraphs   sh   th   ch/tch
wh   ng/nk
	Syllable Types
	    Closed Open
	    Final e Vowel Team
	    r-Controlled Consonant + le

Inflectional Endings (and other suffixes)	Prefixes
OTHER	

The Megabook of Spelling: Grades K–2 © Wiley Blevins, Scholastic Inc.

Section 3
Cumulative Spelling Sentences

Kindergarten

Short *a*
1. I am _____.
2. I sat.

Short *i*
1. Tim sat.
2. The cat is big!

Short *o*
1. I sat on top.
2. Can a big cat hop?

Short *u*
1. We can run in the sun.
2. The big bug can hop.

Short *e*
1. The fat bug is red.
2. Can you get on top of it?

Grade 1

Short *a*
1. Dad has a tan bag.
2. The man sat in the cab.
3. The cat had a nap in the van.

Short *i*
1. Will Sam fix the rip?
2. It is a big pig!
3. Did Jan miss the kick?

Short *o*
1. Did the cat hop on the rock?
2. The lid on the pot is hot!
3. Tom has a big box.

Short *u*
1. The sun is not up.
2. The bus is stuck in the mud.
3. Did the tan bug hop on Liz?

Short *e*
1. The mom hen has ten eggs.
2. Jim has red dots on his legs.
3. Did Ken zip it up yet?

Consonant Blends (*l*-blends)
1. Slip on the sled down the hill.
2. We have six black clocks.
3. Our class has a flat red flag.

Consonant Blends (*s*-blends)
1. Did you spill the glass of milk?
2. We plan to get a snack after we swim.
3. Stop and smell the plant.

Consonant Blends (*r*-blends)
1. Brad has a black truck.
2. Fran went on a grand trip.
3. I saw a crab and frog when I swam.

Digraph *sh*
1. The fish swim fast in the pond.
2. Mom got six black trash bags.
3. I wish to get a little ship at the shop.

Digraph *th*
1. This math game is fun!
2. That big fish swims with its kids.
3. Is the brush thick or thin?

Digraph *ch* and Trigraph *tch*
1. I want fish and chips for lunch.
2. Can you catch this ball?
3. Check how much wood you must chop.

Digraph *wh*
1. When is my bath?
2. Which shop do Chuck and Beth like best?
3. Fran felt the wind whiz by her.

Digraph *ng* and Blend *nk*
1. The king likes to sing songs.
2. Is that a pink fish?
3. The red ring fell in the sink.

Final *e*
1. I hate my black hat!
2. Dave and Hope ride a bus home.
3. Steve has a cute pet snake.

Section 3
Cumulative Spelling Sentences

Long *a*
1. Jay ran to the train.
2. Do you like to play in the rain?
3. We must stay on the main path.

Long *e*
1. We need to sleep all day!
2. I like to eat green beans and peas.
3. Did you see three gray fish at the beach?

Long *o*
1. Is that a green goat on a train?
2. I hope you can play in the snow.
3. Coach Dean told me to go slow.

Long *i*
1. My black kite can fly high.
2. I don't mind if it snows at night.
3. Do I go right or left on this street?

Long *u*
1. Why is that dog so cute?
2. I might need to try it a few times.
3. Does rock music help a plant grow?

r-Controlled Vowels *er, ir, ur*
1. Her sister is in the first grade.
2. Go slow and turn right here.
3. Did the cute bird fly to its nest?

r-Controlled Vowel *ar*
1. Mark has a red barn on his farm.
2. Did you get dirt on your shirt at the park?
3. A nurse shark has so many sharp teeth!

r-Controlled Vowels *or, ore, oar, oor, our*
1. I need more paint for the doors.
2. Did Bart score four goals at the game?
3. Can a goat or a bird roar?

r-Controlled Vowels *air, ear, ere, are*
1. Did the three black bears scare you?
2. Put the four green chairs over there.
3. Do you care if you see a shark at the beach?

Diphthong *oi/oy*
1. That boy has more toy bears than her.
2. I need a pencil with a sharp point.
3. Join me for my third game of checkers.

Diphthong *ou/ow*
1. The boy lives over there in a brown house.
2. We found large bright stars in the sky.
3. My town sits at the mouth of a river.

Complex Vowel /ô/ *a, au, aw*
1. We will walk to the baseball park.
2. Call me because we need to talk.
3. I saw a black hawk fly around.

Short *oo*
1. Look at my book about drawing.
2. We play football in the backyard at my house.
3. That boy will cook a good meal for his mom.

Long *oo* (*oo, ew, ue, u_e*)
1. That blue broom is made of wood.
2. My tooth hurts when I chew food. Ouch!
3. Is it true that we go to the small pool in June?

Section 3
Cumulative Spelling Sentences

Grade 2

**Consonant Blends
(3-letter and complex blends)**
1. My street is full of flowers in the springtime.
2. The mouse let out a quiet squeal.
3. It's a thrill to scream when watching a scary show.
4. We had fun twisting and splashing in the pool.
5. (Teacher's choice)

Digraph *sh*
1. Put the eggshells in the trash.
2. That shark has very sharp teeth!
3. My best friend had fun shopping at the new store.
4. How did that fish vanish so quickly in the pond?
5. (Teacher's choice)

Digraph *th*
1. Beth thinks math is the best subject!
2. Both of those things are true.
3. Tell them to gather thirteen dishes.
4. My tooth hurts when I drink a cold shake.
5. (Teacher's choice)

Digraph *ch* and Trigraph *tch*
1. We all ate fish sandwiches and chips for lunch.
2. My mom and sister wore matching shirts.
3. I think a day at the beach is so much fun!
4. I need to scratch that itch!
5. (Teacher's choice)

Digraph *wh*
1. We went whale watching last week.
2. Where will we go shopping for new shoes?
3. When did the workers wash the windows?
4. A flock of white birds landed on the beach.
5. (Teacher's choice)

Digraph *ng* and Blend *nk*
1. The king likes singing loud songs!
2. Do you think pink is a great color for a ring?
3. Thank you for helping me clean the sink.
4. Please bring over the sandwiches and cold drinks.
5. (Teacher's choice)

Final *e*
1. Steve made a big mistake!
2. Why did Mike's can explode?
3. A snake is a reptile that lives outside.
4. Did that cute hamster escape from its cage?
5. (Teacher's choice)

Long *a*
1. Do you like playing in the rain?
2. Those trains are running on delay.
3. Stay away from that wet paintbrush!
4. May waited a long time for Eve to repay her.
5. (Teacher's choice)

Long *e*
1. Can you repeat that game all week?
2. My team daydreams about winning each match.
3. We agreed to keep eating Mom's green beans.
4. Please don't sneeze near me, Jay!
5. (Teacher's choice)

Long *o*
1. We have hot oatmeal in our bowls.
2. That railroad has very slow trains!
3. It is so cold when it snows all week.
4. Joan grows wheat to make homemade bread.
5. (Teacher's choice)

Long *i*
1. Does the moon give off light at nighttime?
2. Mom might try to make a pie for each child.
3. We must find the right time to meet tonight.
4. Why does Dean like that bright yellow coat?
5. (Teacher's choice)

Long *u*
1. Five cute kittens jumped and played.
2. Which kind of music do you like best?
3. How many pupils are in your class today?
4. I might eat a few bites of that sandwich for lunch.
5. (Teacher's choice)

r-Controlled Vowels *er*, *ir*, *ur*
1. I never gave that yellow shirt to my sister.
2. Did that nice girl return to class yet?
3. We might observe a bird in its nest today.
4. The green bus is turning right at the stoplight.
5. (Teacher's choice)

r-Controlled Vowel *ar*
1. Mark has a huge barn on his farm.
2. Are sharks helpful or harmful in the sea?
3. We spotted a few bright stars in the sky.
4. The market near the park is so much fun to visit!
5. (Teacher's choice)

r-Controlled Vowels *or*, *ore*, *oar*, *oor*, *our*
1. We boarded the bus before it started raining.
2. We need four more singers to perform in the play.
3. Our floors got wet from the storm last night.
4. Our teacher asked us to write a report about birds.
5. (Teacher's choice)

r-Controlled Vowels *air*, *ear*, *ere*, *are*
1. Please be careful when you walk downstairs.
2. I had a nightmare that a bear chased me.
3. Can Mark repair my four broken chairs?
4. Where do you need to wear a coat in the summer?
5. (Teacher's choice)

Diphthong *oi/oy*
1. Parker enjoys wearing shorts when it's very hot.
2. Plant the seeds carefully in the soil.
3. Did that boy spoil his dinner by eating a snack?
4. Come join our team selling corn at the farmer's market.
5. (Teacher's choice)

Diphthong *ou/ow*
1. The boys ran around town to find more chairs.
2. Those brown birds fly south in the winter.
3. At sundown the mouse snuck out of its little house.
4. The clown's huge red frown scared my sister!
5. (Teacher's choice)

Complex Vowel /ô/ *a*, *au*, *aw*
1. We were walking and talking around the school.
2. Joy caught the baseball three times in the game.
3. Did that small rocket launch into space?
4. The girls enjoyed watching the hawk fly high.
5. (Teacher's choice)

Short *oo*
1. Look in the cookbook for a good meal to make for dinner.
2. Joan found my lost notebook in the park.
3. Is football more fun than soccer?
4. Paul understood how to push and pull the taffy.
5. (Teacher's choice)

Section 3

Cumulative Spelling Sentences

Section 3
Cumulative Spelling Sentences

Long oo (oo, ew, ue, u_e)
1. It's true that I got a new blue balloon.
2. Ruth took a bus into town for the afternoon.
3. We helped clean the bathrooms at school.
4. June is a good month to walk in the park.
5. (Teacher's choice)

Silent Letters
1. I know how to climb a tree.
2. I hit my thumb. Ouch!
3. Can you write a story about two friends?
4. Did you wrap that gift at home?
5. (Teacher's choice)

Prefixes un-, re-
1. Is it unsafe to climb a ladder?
2. We need to rewrap the present now.
3. Please unlock the door for us.
4. The teacher is unhappy that we had to retake the test.
5. (Teacher's choice)

Suffix -ing
1. Do you like singing at school?
2. Shopping is more fun than sitting at home!
3. We are taking a break now for lunch.
4. We are saving boxes to make a fort.
5. (Teacher's choice)

Suffix -ed
1. The baseball game ended in a tie.
2. She closed the door and left home.
3. We jumped rope and kicked balls at recess.
4. Kate tripped over those boxes.
5. (Teacher's choice)

Suffixes -ful, -less
1. It is not helpful to feel hopeless.
2. That flu shot was painless.
3. I am thankful we had a rainless weekend.
4. Was the boy careful or careless with the paint?
5. (Teacher's choice)

Suffixes -y, -ly
1. I mostly like funny shows on TV.
2. That is clearly an itchy scrape on your arm.
3. Barb and Joy rarely have messy desks.
4. We ate freshly picked peaches.
5. (Teacher's choice)

Compound Words
1. Do cowboys like to play baseball?
2. We went downtown to get milkshakes.
3. She left her yellow notebook in the lunchroom.
4. We spotted a rainbow over the treetops.
5. (Teacher's choice)

Final Stable Syllables
(*tion, sion, ture, sure*)
1. Is that a picture of a treasure box?
2. That creature measured fifty feet long!
3. Pay attention to hear the directions.
4. I need glasses because my vision is weak.
5. (Teacher's choice)

Closed Syllables
1. Give the basket of muffins to your teacher.
2. I admit that I like going to the dentist.
3. We won the sandwich-making contest.
4. Where is my plastic pencil?
5. (Teacher's choice)

Section 3
Cumulative Spelling Sentences

Open Syllables

1. My hands feel frozen without my mittens.
2. Tell me a secret you recently heard.
3. Can you locate where that music is coming from?
4. The pilot took a photo of the rainbow.
5. (Teacher's choice)

r-Controlled Vowel Syllables

1. My barber has a shop in the market.
2. Garlic tastes perfect in most foods.
3. Which chapter in the book are you reading?
4. Do not disturb me during the soccer game.
5. (Teacher's choice)

Vowel Team Syllables

1. The railroad tracks were covered in snow.
2. Don't complain if you forgot your raincoat.
3. Put the book display in the front window.
4. Do you put mushrooms in your oatmeal?
5. (Teacher's choice)

Consonant + le Syllables

1. Put the bowl of apples in the middle of the table.
2. Are you able to solve this puzzle?
3. Get your rainboots and jump in the puddle!
4. We read a fable about a huge eagle.
5. (Teacher's choice)

Final-e Syllables

1. Complete the test alone.
2. Is a snake a reptile?
3. The athlete made a mistake and lost the game.
4. We will invite him to compete in the singing contest.
5. (Teacher's choice)

Principle 4: Daily Spelling and Writing Activities

Skills Practiced

Phonemic Awareness

Handwriting

Spelling

Decoding

Dictation

Writing

SECTION 4

Word-Building Chains

Word building is a routine in which children build a series of words using letter cards (or on a dry-erase board). Each word in the series, or word chain, varies slightly. It is an ideal activity for assisting children in becoming flexible using the taught sound-spellings.

This activity combines three aspects of learning how words work:

1. high-level phonemic awareness, as children orally manipulate and segment sounds in words
2. encoding/spelling, as they write or build the word using letter cards
3. decoding/reading, as they read their completed word to confirm it's correct

There are two types of word building—blending focus and word-awareness focus—each with a clearly defined instructional purpose. You might dictate the word-building chains early in the instructional cycle and use the blending-focus routine, then repeat the word-building chains later in the instructional cycle and use the word-awareness routine.

Note: A blending focus is best at the beginning of the week when you have just introduced the new phonics skill to children. Then, progress to a word-awareness focus, which provides guided opportunities for children to use both the new phonics skill and previously taught skills flexibly.

For Learners Below Grade-Level Expectations

Try this alternative for children below grade-level expectations: List spelling patterns for the week on the board during this time and have children work with partners to add letters to create words (e.g., __ain, __ain, __ay, __ay). This task is less demanding yet still requires them to practice the on-level target skill to read and write some words. Conduct quick (e.g., 5 minutes) small-group word-building sessions once or twice throughout the week for below-level students to do additional word chains that contain skills with which they need support.

For Multilingual Learners

Provide articulation and vocabulary support throughout the word-building chain. For example, if a child writes *n* instead of *m*, pronounce the /m/ sound and ask the child: *Are my lips together or apart?* (They are together.) Then pronounce the /n/ sound and ask the child: *Are my lips together or apart?* (They are apart.) Continue: *When my lips are together, I write* **m**.

In addition, quickly define words in the word chain. For example: *Say* **sway**. (Pause for children to repeat.) *The word* **sway** *means "to move back and forth." Watch as I* **sway**. (Act it out.) *What have you seen* **sway** *in the wind? Tell your partner.*

All the words in the chains need to be contextualized using actions, objects (realia), or pictures.

Section 4
Word-Building Chains

Materials Needed	The following pages provide guided practice in increasing flexibility with spelling patterns through word building with the target skill, with the target and previously taught skills, and with challenge skills. • Pages 111–112 focus on word chains for kindergarten. • Pages 113–118 provide word chains for Grade 1. • Pages 119–127 feature multisyllabic word chains for Grade 2. **Optional:** letter cards • pocket chart • dry-erase boards and markers
Length of Activity	10 minutes
Location	school or home

Word-Building Routine: Blending Focus

Use the following word-building routine for the differentiated word-building chains provided.

Routine Steps	Sample Teacher Talk
Step 1: Introduce Name the task and explain its purpose to children.	*Today we will be building, or making, words using the letters and spellings we have learned.*
Step 2: Model Place letter cards in a pocket chart (or use letter cards on a whiteboard) to form the first word you are building. You can also do this using a digital whiteboard resource. Model sounding out the word. Remember to: (a) build words using the new target sound-spelling; (b) add words to review sound-spellings as appropriate to extend the practice and application of these skills to achieve mastery; and (c) use minimal contrasts to require children to analyze words fully and notice their unique differences (e.g., *sat* and *mat*, *pan* and *pen*, *rip* and *trip*, *hat* and *hate*, *cot* and *coat*).	*Look at the word I've made. It is spelled* **s-a-t**. *Let's blend the sounds together to read the word:* /sssaaat/, **sat**. *The word is* **sat**. **Note:** The series of words used in a word-building activity is also referred to as a *word chain*.
Step 3: Guided Practice/Practice Continue by having children change one (or more) letters in the word (blending focus). Have children chorally blend the new word formed. Do a set of eight to 10 words as time permits.	*Using your letter cards, change the letter* **s** *in* **sat** *to* **m**. *What is the new word?* Or, if children are more advanced in their understanding, say: *Change the first sound in* **sat** *to* /m/.

Section 4
Word-Building Chains

Word-Building Routine: Word-Awareness Focus

Use the following word-building routine for the differentiated word-building chains provided.

Routine Steps	Sample Teacher Talk
Step 1: Introduce Name the task and explain its purpose to children.	*Today we will be building, or making, words using the letters and spellings we have learned.*
Step 2: Model Place letter cards in a pocket chart (or use letter cards on a whiteboard) to form the first word you are building. You can also do this using a digital whiteboard resource. Model sounding out the word. Remember to: (a) build words using the new target sound spelling; (b) add words to review sound-spellings as appropriate to extend the practice and application of these skills to achieve mastery; and (c) use minimal contrasts to require children to analyze words fully and notice their unique differences (e.g., *sat* and *mat*, *pan* and *pen*, *rip* and *trip*, *hat* and *hate*, *cot* and *coat*).	*Look at the word I've made. It is spelled* **s-a-t**. *Let's blend the sounds together to read the word: /**sssaaat**/,* **sat**. *The word is* **sat**. **Note:** The series of words used in a word building activity is also referred to as a *word chain*.
Step 3: Guided Practice/Practice Continue by stating the next word in the word chain and having children decide what letter or letters must be changed. Have children chorally blend the new word formed. Do a set of eight to 10 words as time permits.	*Using your letter cards, change the word* **sat** *to* **mat**. *What is the new word?* When the focus on word building is word awareness, tell children the next word in the sequence and give them time to form the new word. Circulate and provide assistance and corrective feedback (e.g., modeling your thinking process, modeling how to segment or blend the word). Then build the new word in the pocket chart (or on the whiteboard), modeling aloud your thinking.

Note: When time is tight or the children are in the front of the room on the carpet (instead of at their desks), conduct word building using dry-erase boards. Children erase the part of the word that needs to be changed, then insert the new "missing" letter or spelling. Record the words built on chart paper or the board as you build them for children to self-correct. Then read the entire list of words built at the end from the chart paper to conclude the lesson.

Kindergarten

Consonants and Short Vowels

Word Chain for Target Skill ONLY	Word Chain for Target Skill and Review Skills	Word Chain for Target Skill, Review Skills, and Challenge Words
Target Skill: Short *a*		
at, sat, mat, fat, cat, bat	<not applicable>	at, sat, mat, mad, sad, had, hat, bat, fat, cat, can
Target Skill: Short *i*		
it, sit, fit, bit, big, dig	it, sit, sat, fat, fit, bit, bat, bag, big, dig	**(Plurals)** it, sit, sat, fat, fit, bit, bat, bats, bags, bag, big, dig, digs **(Blends)** hit, bit, lit, lip, slip, flip, flap, clap, cap, lap, tap, tip, rip, trip, drip
Target Skill: Short *o*		
mop, top, hop, hot, not, lot	mop, map, tap, top, tip, hip, hop, hot, hat, cat, cot, lot, not	**(Blends)** mop, map, tap, top, tip, hip, hop, hot, hat, cat, cot, lot, lock, block, clock **(Digraphs)** mop, map, tap, top, tip, hip, ship, shop, chop, hop, hot, hat, chat, that
Target Skill: Short *u*		
up, cup, cut, but, bun, fun, sun, run	up, cup, cut, cot, cat, bat, bit, but, bun, ban, fan, fin, fun, sun, run, ran	**(Blends)** up, cup, cut, cat, cap, clap, slap, slip, flip, lip, rip, drip, trip, trap, track, truck, tuck, stuck, stick, sick, lick, luck, lock **(Digraphs)** up, cup, cap, cat, cut, hut, shut, hut, hot, shot, shop, chop, chip, chin, thin, tin, tan, fan, fun, run, sun

Section 4
Word-Building Chains

Section 4
Word-Building Chains

Word Chains: Kindergarten

Word Chain for Target Skill ONLY	Word Chain for Target Skill and Review Skills	Word Chain for Target Skill, Review Skills, and Challenge Words
Target Skill: Short e		
red, bed, bet, let, get, wet, web	red, bed, bad, bat, bit, bet, let, get, got, hot, hat, hit, hut, nut, not, net, wet, web	**(Blends)** red, bed, bled, sled, fled, led, lad, bad, bat, bit, bet, let, get, got, hot, hat, hit, hut, nut, not, net, wet, web
		(Digraphs and Blends) red, bed, bled, sled, shed, sped, spend, spent, sent, went, wet, wit, wish, fish, dish, dash, lash, flash, rash, crash, trash, track

Grade 1

Section 4
Word-Building Chains

Word Chain for Target Skill ONLY	Word Chain for Target Skill and Review Skills	Word Chain for Target Skill, Review Skills, and Challenge Words
Target Skill: Short *a*		
mat, sat, cat, hat, had, mad, map, man, can, cat, sat, sad, bad, dad	<not applicable>	mat, sat, cat, chat, hat, had, mad, map, man, can, cans, cats, cat, sat, sad, bad, dad
Target Skill: Short *i*		
bin, win, tin, fin, fit, hit, hid, did, dig, dim, dip, tip, sip	bin, win, tin, tan, fan, fin, fit, hit, hat, had, hid, did, dig, dim, dip, tip, tap, sap, sip	bin, win, pin, spin, pin, tin, tan, fan, fin, fit, hit, hat, had, hid, did, dig, dim, dip, lip, slip, slap, lap, tap, sap, sip, snip, snap
Target Skill: Short *o*		
not, lot, pot, pop, hop, hot, dot, got, gob, rob, rock, sock	not, lot, lit, hit, hat, pat, pot, pop, pip, hip, hop, hot, dot, got, gob, rob, rock, rack, sack, sock	not, lot, lit, hit, hot, shot, hot, hat, pat, pot, spot, pot, pop, pip, hip, ship, shop, hop, hot, dot, got, gob, rob, rock, rack, sack, stack, stock, sock, shock
Target Skill: Short *u*		
sun, bun, run, rub, cub, cup, cut, nut, hut, hug, bug, rug, tug, tuck, luck	sun, bun, bin, ban, ran, run, rub, cub, cob, cop, cup, cut, nut, not, hot, hut, hug, bug, bag, big, rig, rug, tug, tuck, tack, tock, lock, luck	sun, bun, bin, ban, ran, run, rub, cub, club, cub, cob, cop, cup, cut, nut, not, hot, shot, shut, hut, hug, bug, bag, big, rig, rug, tug, tuck, stuck, stack, tack, tock, lock, clock, cluck, luck, lick, slick, stick
Target Skill: Short *e*		
hen, ten, pen, pet, let, leg, beg, bet, net, wet, web, well, sell, tell	hen, ten, tin, tan, pan, pen, pin, pit, pat, pot, pet, let, leg, beg, bag, bat, bet, bot, not, net, wet, web, well, sell, tell	hen, when, then, ten, tin, tan, pan, pen, pin, spin, spit, pit, pat, pot, spot, pot, pet, let, leg, beg, bag, bat, bet, bot, not, hot, shot, spot, pot, pet, net, wet, web, well, tell, sell, spell, shell

Word Chains: Grade 1

Section 4
Word-Building Chains

Word Chain for Target Skill ONLY	Word Chain for Target Skill and Review Skills	Word Chain for Target Skill, Review Skills, and Challenge Words
Target Skill: Consonant Blends (*l*-blends)		
lip, flip, clip, slip, slap, clap, flap, flag, flat	lip, flip, flap, clap, clip, slip, lip, lap, slap, slop, flop, flap, flag, flat, fat	lip, flip, flap, clap, clip, chip, hip, ship, slip, lip, lap, slap, slop, flop, flap, flag, flat, fat
Target Skill: Consonant Blends (*s*-blends)		
lid, slid, slip, slim, slick, sick, stick, stack, stuck	lid, slid, slip, slim, slick, sick, stick, stack, stuck, tuck, truck, track, trap, trip, drip, drop	lid, slid, slip, slim, slick, sick, stick, stack, stuck, tuck, truck, track, trap, trip, drip, drop, shop, chop, chip, ship
Target Skill: Consonant Blends (*r*-blends)		
rip, drip, grip, trip, trap, tap, top, drop, crop, crib, crab	rip, drip, grip, trip, tip, rip, rap, trap, tap, top, tip, rip, drip, drop, crop, crib, crab	rip, drip, grip, trip, tip, chip, ship, rip, rap, trap, tap, top, shop, chop, hop, hip, tip, rip, drip, drop, crop, crib, crab
Target Skill: Digraph *sh*		
hop, shop, ship, shin, win, fin, fish, wish, dish, dash, cash	hop, shop, ship, shin, win, fin, fish, wish, dish, dash, cash, crash, trash	hop, shop, ship, chip, chips, ships, ship, shin, win, thin, fin, fish, wish, with, wish, dish, dash, mash, smash, sash, cash, crash, trash
Target Skill: Digraph *th*		
tin, thin, thick, tick, tin, win, with, math, bath, path	tin, thin, thick, tick, tin, win, with, math, path, bath, both, boat, beat, seat, south	tin, thin, thick, chick, tick, stick, sick, sit, wit, win, with, wish, dish, dash, mash, math, path, bath, both, boat, beat, seat, south
Target Skill: Digraph *ch* and Trigraph *tch*		
hop, chop, chap, chip, chin, win, with, witch *(person)*, pitch, patch, catch	hop, chop, chap, chip, chin, win, with, witch *(person)*, pitch, patch, catch, cash, crash, trash, trap, trip, tip, hip, harp, hard, card, cart, chart, part, port, sport	hop, chop, chap, chip, chin, win, with, witch *(person)*, pitch, patch, patches, catches, catch, cash, crash, trash, trap, trip, tip, hip, harp, hard, card, cart, chart, part, port, sport, sports, sporty

Word Chains: Grade 1

Section 4
Word-Building Chains

Word Chain for Target Skill ONLY	Word Chain for Target Skill and Review Skills	Word Chain for Target Skill, Review Skills, and Challenge Words
Target Skill: Digraph *wh*		
when, which, whip, whiz, why, what, where	when, which, whip, whiz, why, what, where, there, then, thin, think, thank	when, which, whip, whiz, why, what, where, there, then, thin, think, thinking, thanking, thank, thankful, thankless
Target Skill: Digraph *ng* and Blend *nk*		
win, wing, wink, sink, think, thing, ring, king, sing, sang, sung, sunk	win, wing, wink, sink, think, thing, ring, king, sing, sang, sung, sunk, sank, sand, send, spend, spent, sent, went, vent, vet, vat, van, fan, far, farm, form, firm	win, wing, wink, sink, sinking, thinking, think, thing, ring, ringing, singing, sing, king, sing, sang, sung, sunk, sink, sank, sand, send, sending, spending, spend, spent, sent, went, vent, vet, vat, van, fan, far, farm, form, former, firmer, firm, first
Target Skill: Final *e*		
tap, tape, cape, cap, can, cane, came, cave, save, same	tap, tape, cape, cap, can, cane, came, cave, save, same, game	tap, tape, cape, cap, can, cane, came, cave, save, shave, shame, same, game
hop, hope, rope, rose, nose, nope, note, not	hop, hope, rope, rose, nose, nope, note, not, hot, hat, hate, late, lake	hop, hope, rope, rose, nose, nope, note, not, hot, hat, hate, late, lake, like, liked, liking
cut, cute, cube, cub, hug, huge	cut, cute, cube, cub, hug, huge, home, hope	cut, cute, cube, cub, hug, huge, hug, hugging, hugged
bit, bite, bike, like, life, lime, time, dime, dim	bit, bite, bike, bake, lake, like, life, lime, time, dime, dim	bit, bite, bike, bake, lake, like, life, lime, slime, lime, time, dime, dive, drive, drove
Target Skill: Long *a*		
ran, rain, main, pain, pan, pay, way, say, ray	ran, rain, main, man, tan, pan, pain, paint, pant, pan, pay, way, say, ray	ran, rain, train, training, raining, rain, main, man, tan, pan, pain, paint, painting, paint, pant, pants, pans, pan, pay, pays, ways, way, say, sway, stay, stray, tray, ray

Section 4
Word-Building Chains

Word Chains: Grade 1

Word Chain for Target Skill ONLY	Word Chain for Target Skill and Review Skills	Word Chain for Target Skill, Review Skills, and Challenge Words
Target Skill: Long e		
met, meat, neat, seat, set, pet, pen, men, mean, bean	met, meat, neat, net, set, seat, set, pet, pen, pan, man, men, mean, main, rain, ran, ban, Ben, bean	met, meat, neat, net, set, seat, set, pet, pen, pan, man, men, mean, main, rain, train, brain, bran, ban, Ben, bean
feed, feel, feet, feed, seed, need	feed, feel, feet, feed, fed, red, bed, bead, beat, heat, hat, bat, bet, bed, fed, feed, seed	feed, feel, feet, sheet, shot, shop, shed, fed, red, bed, bled, bleed, bead, beat, heat, hat, bat, bet, bed, fed, feed, seed, speed
Target Skill: Long o		
got, goat, boat, bat, cat, coat, coal, goal	got, goat, boat, bat, cat, coat, coal, goal, go, so, no	got, goat, boat, boats, boat, bat, cat, coat, coal, goal, goals
lot, low, row, mow	lot, low, row, mow, mown (*grass*), moan (*sound*), main, mean, meat, met, bet, bat, bot, boat, bow, bowl	lot, low, slow, show, showing, rowing, row, mow, mowing, mown (*grass*), moan (*sound*), main, mean, meat, met, bet, bat, bot, boat, bow, bowl, bowling
Target Skill: Long i		
lit, light, night, right, sight, sit	lit, light, night, right, sight, sit, sat, set, seat, meat (*food*), meet (*person*), feet, fight, fit	lit, light, slight, sight, night, right, bright, right, sight, sit, sat, set, seat, meat (*food*), meet (*person*), feet, fight, fit, flit, flight, fright
fine, find, mind, mine	fine, find, mind, mine, line, lane	fine, find, mind, mine, pine, spine, shine
my, by, why	my, by, why, shy, show, grow, go, got, hot, hat, heat	my, by, try, cry, dry, why, shy, show, grow, go, got, hot, hat, heat, cheat, wheat
Target Skill: Long u		
cut, cute, cube, cub, hub, hug, huge, fuse, few, view	cut, cute, cube, cub, hub, hug, huge, mute, muse, fuse, few, view	cut, cute, cube, cub, hub, hug, huge, fuse, few, view, review, preview

The Megabook of Spelling: Grades K–2

Word Chains: Grade 1

Section 4 — Word-Building Chains

Word Chain for Target Skill ONLY	Word Chain for Target Skill and Review Skills	Word Chain for Target Skill, Review Skills, and Challenge Words
Target Skill: r-Controlled Vowels er, ir, ur		
nerve, serve, swerve	nerve, serve, swerve, swell	nerve, serve, swerve, swerved, swerving
girl, twirl, swirl	girl, twirl, swirl, swim	girl, twirl, twirling, swirling, swirl, swirled, twirled
cub, curb, curl, burn, turn	cub, curb, curl, curt, turn, burn, bun, bean, mean, main, moan	cub, curb, curl, curling, curl, curt, turn, turning, turned, burned, burn, bun, bean, mean, main, moan, moaning
Target Skill: r-Controlled Vowel ar		
car, card, cart, dart, dark, park, part, pat, par, far, farm	car, card, cart, dart, dark, park, part, pat, par, far, farm, firm, first, thirst, third	car, card, cards, carts, cart, dart, dark, park, part, pat, par, far, farm, farmer, firmer, firm, first, thirst, thirsty, thirty, third
Target Skill: r-Controlled Vowels or, ore		
for, form, fork, fort, port, pork, cork, core, more, wore, sore, tore, torn, born	for, form, farm, harm, hard, card, cord, cork, fork, fort, port, part, park, pork, cork, core, more, wore, sore, tore, torn, born	for, form, former, farmer, farm, harm, hard, card, cord, cork, fork, fort, port, part, park, pork, cork, core, more, wore, sore, tore, store, storm, form, worm (/ûr/), worn, torn, born, barn, burn, burning, turning
Target Skill: r-Controlled Vowels air, ear, ere, are		
hair, chair, fair,* fare,* care, bare,* bear,* tear, wear,* where,* there (* Provide meaning clues)	hair, chair, fair,* fare,* far, car, care, share, bare,* bear,* bar, tar, tear, wear,* where,* there (* Provide meaning clues)	hair, chair, chairs, fairs, fair,* fare,* far, farm, harm, hard, card, car, care, share, bare,* bear,* bar, tar, tear, wear,* where,* wherever, wherefore, therefore, there (* Provide meaning clues)
Target Skill: Diphthong oi/oy		
boy, toy, soy, joy, join, soil	boy, boys, toys, toy, soy, say, jay, joy, join, joins, jeans, beans, bean, mean, meal, seal, soil	boy, boys, cowboys, boys, toys, toy, soy, say, jay, joy, enjoy, joyful, joy, join, rejoin, rejoins, joins, jeans, beans, bean, mean, meal, seal, soil, moist, moisture

Section 4
Word-Building Chains

Word Chains: Grade 1

Word Chain for Target Skill ONLY	Word Chain for Target Skill and Review Skills	Word Chain for Target Skill, Review Skills, and Challenge Words
Target Skill: Diphthong ou/ow		
cow, now, wow, pow, pout, pound, round, sound, south	cow, now, wow, pow, pout, pound, round, sound, south, mouth, moth, math, bath, bat, beat, seat, meat, mart, mark, marker	cow, now, wow, pow, powwow, pout, pound, round, rounder, sound, south, mouth, moth, math, bath, bat, beat, seat, meat, mart, mark, marker, market, marking, parking, park, perk, pork
Target Skill: Complex Vowel /ô/ a, au, aw		
all, ball, call, fall, tall, talk, walk, wall, hall, halt, salt, saw, jaw, paw, pause	all, ball, call, fall, fell, tell, tall, talk, walk, wall, fall, fill, hill, hall, halt, salt, saw, jaw, paw, pawn, dawn, down, town, torn	all, ball, baseball, ball, call, calling, falling, fall, fell, tell, tall, taller, talker, talk, walk, wall, fall, fill, hill, hall, halt, salt, saw, jaw, paw, pawn, dawn, down, town, torn, worn, work, worker
Target Skill: Short oo		
book, cook, look, hook, hoof, hood, good	book, cook, look, lock, shock, shook, hook, hoof, hood, good	book, cookbook, cook, cooking, looking, look, lock, locker, shocker, shock, shook, hook, hoof, hood, good
Target Skill: Long oo (oo, ew, ue, u_e)		
room, roof, root, boot	room, roof, root, boot, boat, beat	room, bedroom, room, roof, root, boot, booth, tooth, teeth, team, seam, seat, beat, boat
new, grew, flew	new, grew, flew, flow, glow	new, grew, flew, flow, flown, grown, green
clue, blue, glue, true	clue, blue, glue, true, tree, street	clue, blue, glue, true, tree, street, treat, trout
tub, tube, tune, June	tub, tube, tune, June, Jane	tub, tube, tune, June, July
Target Skill: Silent Letters		
know, knot, knob	know, knot, knob, knee	know, knowing, know, knot, knotted, knot, knob
gnat, gnaw, gnash	gnat, gnaw, gnash, trash	gnat, gnaw, gnawing, gnashing, gnash, trash, trashcan
wrote, write, wrist	wrote, write, white, wit, wrist	wrote, write, white, wit, wrist, written

Grade 2
Multisyllabic Words

Letter Cards	Word Chain	Extension
Target Skill: Consonant Blends (3-letter and complex blends)		
a, i, o, u, b, c, g, l, ll, n, p, r, s, t	tip, trip, strip, strap, scrap, scrub, scroll, stroll, strong, string, spring, sprint, splint, split	Contextualize words by focusing on vocabulary. Provide an image/illustration or object, act out the word, or briefly define and connect the word to a simpler known word. When possible, use a translation app to share the word in the children's home language as well.

Syllable Cards	Word Chain	Extension
Target Skill: Final e		
in, ways, walk, cup, pan, less, side, cake, life, time	inside, sideways, sidewalk, cupcake, pancake, lifetime, timeless	Discuss about morphology; for example, explain how we can often (but not always) use the meanings of the smaller words in a **compound word** to determine the meaning of the whole compound word.
		Contextualize words by focusing on vocabulary. Provide an image/illustration or object, act out the word, or briefly define and connect the word to a simpler known word. When possible, use a translation app to share the word in the children's home language as well.

Word Chains: Grade 2

Section 4
Word-Building Chains

Syllable Cards	Word Chain	Extension
Target Skill: Long *a*		
ing, ed, un, re, train, play, paid, paint, pay	retrain, retrained, untrained, training, playing, played, unpaid, repaid, repaint, repainting, repainted, repay, paying	Discuss about morphology; for example, focus on the meanings of the **prefixes** (*un* = not, opposite of; *re* = again) and **suffixes** (*ed* = past tense; *ing* = present). Point out when the prefix or suffix is a separate syllable. Address any spelling changes (change *y* to *i*) needed when adding a suffix.
Target Skill: Long *e*		
ing, ed, un, re, clean, heat, read, sleep, freeze	cleaned, cleaning, recleaning, rereading, reading, sleeping, heating, reheating, reheated, unheated, unheat, reheat, refreeze, freeze	Discuss about morphology; for example, focus on the meanings of the **prefixes** (*un* = not, opposite of; *re* = again) and **suffixes** (*ed* = past tense; *ing* = present). Point out when the prefix or suffix is a separate syllable.
Target Skill: Long *o*		
ing, ed, er, est, un, re, roll, sold, load, roast, grow, slow, cold	rolling, rolled, rerolled, unrolled, unsold, resold, reload, reloading, unloading, unloaded, loaded, roasted, roasting, growing, regrowing, regrow, grow, grower, slower, slowest, coldest, colder, cold	Discuss about morphology; for example, focus on the meanings of the **prefixes** (*un* = not, opposite of; *re* = again) and **suffixes** (*ed* = past tense; *ing* = present; *er* = one who; also, compares two things and has two letters; *est* = compares three or more things and has three letters). Point out when the prefix or suffix is a separate syllable.
Target Skill: Long *i*		
ing, er, est, re, light, bright, fight, try, find, mild, wild	lighter, lightest, brightest, brighter, milder, mildest, wildest, wilder, fighter, fighting, finding, trying, retrying	Discuss about morphology; for example, focus on the meanings of the **prefixes** (*re* = again) and **suffixes** (*ing* = present; *er* = one who; also, compares two things and has two letters; *est* = compares three or more things and has three letters). Point out when the prefix or suffix is a separate syllable.

Word Chains: Grade 2

Section 4 — Word-Building Chains

Syllable Cards	Word Chain	Extension
Target Skill: Long u		
ing, ed, er, est, re, pre, unit, view, few	unit, united, viewed, viewing, reviewing, review, preview, view, few, fewer, fewest	Discuss about morphology; for example, focus on the meanings of the **prefixes** (*pre* = before; *re* = again) and **suffixes** (*ed* = past tense; *ing* = present; *er* = compares two things and has two letters; *est* = compares three or more things and has three letters). Point out when the prefix or suffix is a separate syllable.
Target Skill: *r*-Controlled Vowels *er, ir, ur*		
ing, ed, re, un, y, burn, turn, furl, hurt, twirl, whirl, germ	burned, burning, turning, returning, return, turn, turned, furled, unfurled, furl, hurt, unhurt, hurting, twirling, whirling, whirly, twirly, germy	Discuss about morphology; for example, focus on the meanings of the **prefixes** (*re* = again; *un* = not, opposite of) and **suffixes** (*ed* = past tense; *ing* = present; *y* = characterized by). Point out when the prefix or suffix is a separate syllable.
Target Skill: *r*-Controlled Vowel *ar*		
ing, er, est, ful, less, re, farm, harm, charm, dark, hard, start, sharp	farmer, farming, harming, harmful, harmless, harm, hard, harder, hardest, darkest, darker, sharper, starter, starting, restarting, start, charm, charming, charmer, charmless	Discuss about morphology; for example, focus on the meanings of the **prefixes** (*re* = again) and **suffixes** (*ing* = present; *er* = one who; also, comparing two things; *est* = compares three or more things and has three letters; *ful* = full of; *less* = without or lacking). Point out when the prefix or suffix is a separate syllable.
Target Skill: *r*-Controlled Vowels *or, ore*		
ing, ed, im, ex, re, trans, er, able, port	portable, porter, reporter, reporting, reported, report, export, exporting, exported, imported, import, importing, transporting, transported, transportable	Discuss about morphology; for example, focus on the meanings of the **root** (*port* = carry), **prefixes** (*ex* = out; *im* = in; *trans* = across), and **suffixes** (*ed* = past tense; *ing* = present; *er* = one who; *able* = can or able to). Point out when the prefix or suffix is a separate syllable.

Word Chains: Grade 2

Section 4: Word-Building Chains

Syllable Cards	Word Chain	Extension
Target Skill: r-Controlled Vowels *air, ear, ere, are*		
ing, ed, de, re, des, under, outer, clare, pair, wear	declare, despair, repair, repaired, repairing, pairing, wearing, wear, underwear, outerwear	Discuss about morphology; for example, focus on the meanings of the **prefixes** (*under* = underneath; *outer* = outside; *re* = again) and **suffixes** (*ed* = past tense; *ing* = present). Point out when the prefix or suffix is a separate syllable.
Target Skill: Diphthong *oi/oy*		
ing, ed, re, en, over, ful, less, joy, join, boil, broil	boiling, boiled, broiled, broiling, enjoying, enjoyed, enjoy, joyful, joyless, overjoyed, joy, join, rejoin, rejoining, rejoined	Discuss about morphology; for example, focus on the meanings of the **prefixes** (*re* = again; *over* = more than; *en* = in or within) and **suffixes** (*ed* = past tense; *ing* = present; *ful* = full of; *less* = without or lacking). Point out when the prefix or suffix is a separate syllable.
Target Skill: Diphthong *ou/ow*		
town, down, house, fire, boat, break, count, dog, light, sun, touch, out, with, work, hang, look, ing	sundown, breakdown, countdown, touchdown, downtown, townhouse, firehouse, lighthouse, boathouse, doghouse, houseboat, boating, working, workout, without, hangout, lookout	Discuss about morphology; for example, explain how we can often (but not always) use the meanings of the smaller words in a **compound word** to determine the meaning of the whole compound word.
Target Skill: Complex Vowel /ô/ *a, au, aw*		
ball, base, foot, basket, snow, hall, way, walk, board	baseball, football, basketball, snowball, ball, hall, hallway, walkway, boardwalk	Discuss about morphology; for example, explain how we can often (but not always) use the meanings of the smaller words in a **compound word** to determine the meaning of the whole compound word.

Word Chains: Grade 2

Section 4
Word-Building Chains

Syllable Cards	Word Chain	Extension
Target Skill: Short *oo*		
cook, book, foot, took, hood, case, note, bare, ball, mis, child, father, like, li	cookbook, bookcase, notebook, barefoot, football, mistook, childhood, fatherhood, likelihood	Discuss about morphology; for example, explain how we can often (but not always) use the meanings of the smaller words in a **compound word** to determine the meaning of the whole compound word.
Target Skill: Long *oo* (*oo, ew, ue*)		
room, bath, bed, class, zoom, chew, clue, true, glue, ing, ed, less, ful, un	bathroom, bedroom, classroom, room, zoom, zooming, chewing, chew, clue, clueless, truthless, truthful, true, glue, unglue, unglued	Discuss about morphology, such as **compound words** and the meanings of the **prefixes** (*un* = not, opposite of) and **suffixes** (*ed* = past tense; *ing* = present; *ful* = full of; *less* = without or lacking). Point out when the prefix or suffix is a separate syllable and address any spelling changes (drop *e*) needed when adding a suffix.
Target Skill: Silent Letters		
ing, ed, ful, less, know, knock, write, climb, comb, doubt, wrap, wreck	knowing, knocking, writing, climbing, combing, doubting, doubtful, doubtless, doubted, wrapped, wrapping, wrecking, wrecked	Discuss about morphology; for example, focus on the meanings of the **suffixes** (*ed* = past tense; *ing* = present; *ful* = full of; *less* = without or lacking). Point out when the suffix is a separate syllable. Address any spelling changes (drop *e*, double final consonant) needed when adding a suffix.

Word Chains: Grade 2

Section 4
Word-Building Chains

Syllable Cards	Word Chain	Extension
Target Skill: Prefixes *un-*, *re-*		
un, re, ed, born, cover, do, tie, wind, wrap, attach	unborn, reborn, recover, uncover, undo, redo, retie, retied, untied, untie, unwind, rewind, rewrap, unwrap, unwrapped, unattached, reattached	Discuss about morphology; for example, focus on the meanings of the **prefixes** (*re* = again; *un* = not, opposite of) and **suffix** (*ed* = past tense). Point out that the prefix is a separate syllable. Model how to use the prefix to determine the word's meaning. Address any spelling changes (drop *e*, double final consonant) needed when adding a suffix.
Target Skill: Suffix *-ing*		
ing, jump, plant, teach, wash, cry, try, stop, drip, trap, shop	jumping, planting, teaching, washing, crying, trying, stopping, dripping, trapping, shopping	Discuss about morphology; for example, focus on the meaning of the **suffix** (*ing* = present). Point out when the suffix is a separate syllable. Address any spelling changes (double final consonant) needed when adding a suffix.
Target Skill: Suffix *-ed*		
ed, end, melt, fade, code, plot, shred, blame, jog, use, ask, bike, place, brush, step, stop	ended, melted, faded, coded, plotted, shredded, blamed, jogged, used, asked, biked, placed, brushed, stepped, stopped	Discuss about morphology; for example, focus on the meaning of the **suffix** (*ed* = past tense). Point out the three sounds for the suffix *-ed* (/d/, /t/, /ed/). Address any spelling changes (drop *e*, double final consonant) needed when adding a suffix. **Note:** When spelling words with *-ed*, have children first identify the base word. Then prompt them to "add the suffix/ending that makes the word mean something that happened in the past."

Word Chains: Grade 2

Section 4
Word-Building Chains

Syllable Cards	Word Chain	Extension
Target Skill: Suffixes -ful, -less		
ful, less, hope, help, color, care, cheer, pain, thank, use, rest	hopeful, hopeless, helpless, helpful, colorful, colorless, careless, careful, cheerful, cheerless, painless, painful, thankful, thankless, useless, useful, restful, restless	Discuss about morphology; for example, focus on the meanings of the **suffixes** (*ful* = full of; *less* = without or lacking). Point out when the suffix is a separate syllable.
Target Skill: Suffixes -y, -ly		
y, ly, grass, hair, itch, ease, squeak, hill, calm, cost, firm, friend, nice, like	grassy, hairy, itchy, easy, squeaky, hilly, calmly, costly, firmly, friendly, nicely, likely	Discuss about morphology; for example, focus on the meanings of the **suffixes** (*y* = characterized by; *ly* = in a way that is). Point out when the suffix is a separate syllable. Address any spelling changes needed (drop *e*) when adding a suffix.
Target Skill: Compound Words		
back, ground, seat, yard, bath, tub, room, robe, door, bell, knob, way, snow, man, ball, storm, thunder	background, backseat, backyard, bathtub, bathroom, bathrobe, backdoor, doorbell, doorknob, doorway, snowman, snowball, snowstorm, thunderstorm	Discuss about morphology; for example, explain how we can often (but not always) use the meanings of the smaller words in a **compound word** to determine the meaning of the whole compound word.
Target Skill: Final Stable Syllables (*tion, sion, ture, sure*)		
tion, sion, ture, sure, addi, vaca, ero, explo, mea, trea, pic, mix, tex, mois, plea, expo, celebra, defini, televi, inva	addition, vacation, erosion, explosion, measure, treasure, picture, mixture, texture, moisture, pleasure, exposure, celebration, definition, television, invasion	Contextualize words by focusing on vocabulary. Provide an image/illustration or object, act out the word, or briefly define and connect the word to a simpler known word. When possible, use a translation app to share the word in the children's home language as well.

Word Chains: Grade 2

Section 4 — Word-Building Chains

Syllable	Word Chain	Extension
Target Skill: Closed Syllables		
nap, kin, cab, in, sect, kit, ten, mit, hab, it, hid, den, mag, net, den, tist	napkin, cabin, insect, kitten, mitten, habit, hidden, magnet, dentist	Contextualize words by focusing on vocabulary. Provide an image/illustration or object, act out the word, or briefly define and connect the word to a simpler known word. When possible, use a translation app to share the word in the children's home language as well.
Target Skill: Open Syllables		
si, lent, fro, zen, mu, sic, bo, nus, pi, lot, fe, male, ba, con, by, cra, zy, pre, fix	silent, frozen, music, bonus, pilot, female, bacon, baby, crazy, prefix	Contextualize words by focusing on vocabulary. Provide an image/illustration or object, act out the word, or briefly define and connect the word to a simpler known word. When possible, use a translation app to share the word in the children's home language as well.
Target Skill: *r*-Controlled Vowel Syllables		
mar, ket, ble, per, fect, form, for, ty, dir, num, ber, rub, lim, slip, per, win, ter	market, marble, perfect, perform, forty, dirty, number, rubber, limber, slipper, winter	Contextualize words by focusing on vocabulary. Provide an image/illustration or object, act out the word, or briefly define and connect the word to a simpler known word. When possible, use a translation app to share the word in the children's home language as well.
Target Skill: Vowel-Team Syllables		
rail, road, rain, coat, sea, weed, high, light, way, hall, oat, meal, time, ex, plain, com, re, peat, pro, ceed	railroad, raincoat, seaweed, highlight, highway, hallway, oatmeal, mealtime, explain, complain, repeat, proceed	Contextualize words by focusing on vocabulary. Provide an image/illustration or object, act out the word, or briefly define and connect the word to a simpler known word. When possible, use a translation app to share the word in the children's home language as well.

Word Chains: Grade 2

Section 4
Word-Building Chains

Syllable Cards	Word Chain	Extension
Target Skill: Consonant + *le* **Syllables**		
ble, tle, cle, zle, ple, gle, dle, ta, bub, lit, tur, cir, un, puz, fiz, pur, sim, ea, bu, han, rid	table, bubble, little, turtle, circle, uncle, puzzle, fizzle, purple, simple, eagle, bugle, handle, riddle	Contextualize words by focusing on vocabulary. Provide an image/illustration or object, act out the word, or briefly define and connect the word to a simpler known word. When possible, use a translation app to share the word in the children's home language as well.
Target Skill: Final-*e* Syllables		
hope, life, time, side, made, male, vite, plete, lete, tile, pose, less, walk, com, de, un, in, fe, rep, ex	hopeless, lifetime, sidewalk, unmade, female, invite, complete, delete, reptile, expose	Contextualize words by focusing on vocabulary. Provide an image/illustration or object, act out the word, or briefly define and connect the word to a simpler known word. When possible, use a translation app to share the word in the children's home language as well.

Principle 4: Daily Spelling and Writing Activities

Skills Practiced

Phonemic Awareness

Handwriting

Spelling

Decoding

Dictation

Writing

SECTION 5

Word-Sort Sets

Word sorts involve children arranging a set of words, often on individual word cards, into piles or groupings based on common features (e.g., all contain the same vowel sound but with different spellings, as in *ai* and *ay* words for long *a*; all contain a common prefix or suffix; all are nouns or verbs). In a closed sort, you provide the categories into which children will group the words. In an open sort, children determine the categories themselves.

Word sorts allow children time to think about how words work by drawing their attention to important and common spelling patterns or morphological units (e.g., prefixes and suffixes). They offer teachers an opportunity to share and/or reinforce generalizations about how English words work, including details that can aid in spelling (e.g., the *ai* spelling for long *a* appears in the middle of a word and never at the end, whereas the *ay* spelling appears at the end). The learning happens during and after a word sort. Ask children: *What do you notice about these spellings? What did you learn about these spelling patterns?*

Notes About Spelling Generalizations: Rather than teaching unreliable or complicated rules, word sorts offer an opportunity to highlight generalizations about how English words work that can greatly benefit children as they spell. But always present generalizations as "usually" applying and highlight key exceptions to avoid confusion.

Sample Common Generalizations to Point Out During Sorts

See Section 13 (pages 315–320) for additional support.

- The position of spellings in words (e.g., *ai* in the middle, *ay* at the end of long-*a* words; *oi* in the middle, *oy* at the end of diphthong /oi/ words; *oa* in the middle, *ow* at the end or followed by *l*, *n*, *er* in long-*o* words)

- The *igh* spelling is usually followed by the letter *t*.

- The *er* spelling for /ûr/ is common at the end of multisyllabic words (e.g., *never*, *farmer*).

- FLSZ/Floss Rule (double consonants at end of short-vowel words, such as *sniff*, *tell*, *miss*, *buzz*)

- The *ck* spelling for /k/ comes at the end of one-syllable words after short vowels (e.g., *sick*). Otherwise, use the spelling *k* (e.g., after consonant in *sink*, or vowel team in *week*; or at the beginning of some /k/ sound words, as in *ki* [*kick*] and *ke* [*kept*]). Note that the spelling *c* for the sound /k/ is often in words that begin with *ca* (*cat*), *co* (*cot*), and *cu* (*cut*).

- No English word ends with the letter *j* or the letter *v*. If a word ends with the /v/ sound, you must add an *e* (e.g., *have*, *live*). The sound /j/ at the end of a one-syllable word after a single short vowel is often spelled *-dge* (e.g., *fudge*).

- The spelling *-tch* comes at the end of a word after a short vowel, as in *patch*; otherwise, use *-ch*, as in *bench* and *beach*.

- The *y* as the consonant sound /y/ appears at the beginning of a word like *yes*, but as a vowel sound at the end of words (e.g., long-*i* sound, as in *my*, *why*, *try*—one-syllable words; long-*e* sound, as in *happy*, *funny*, *tricky*—two-syllable words).

- Soft *c* and *g* (/s/ and /j/, respectively) usually comes before *e*, *i*, or *y*; but there are notable exceptions, such as *girl*. Focus on the spelling patterns *ce*, *ci*, *cy*, *ge*, *gi*, *gy*.
- The /ûr/ sounds are often spelled *or* after the letter *w*, as in *word* and *work*.
- Related words can help children understand how spellings in base words are maintained across words, such as *sign/signal/signature* (why silent letter *g* is used), *limb/limber* (why silent letter *b* is used), and *different/difference*, *excellent/excellence*, *fragrant/fragrance* (*ent/ence* versus *ant/ance*).

Section 5
Word-Sort Sets

Materials Needed	The following pages provide guided practice in sorting words to focus on key spelling patterns and deepening understanding of how English works. Write each word in a word-sort set on an index card for each child or small group. • Page 131 features differentiated word sorts for kindergarten. • Pages 132–136 provide differentiated word sorts for Grade 1. • Pages 137–142 offer differentiated word sorts for Grade 2.
Length of Activity	10 minutes
Location	school or home

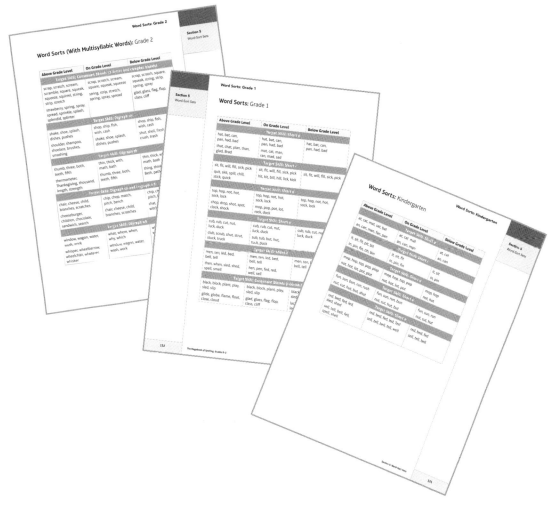

Section 5: Word-Sort Sets

Section 5
Word-Sort Sets

Word-Sort Routine

Use the following word-sort routine for the provided word-sort sets.

Routine Steps	Sample Teacher Talk
Step 1: Introduce Name the task and explain its purpose. Distribute the word cards and read each word with children to make sure they know all of the words. If you are doing a closed sort, introduce the categories in which children will be sorting the words. **Alternative:** List the words on the board for children to record in categories in their writer's notebooks.	*Today, we are going to sort words into two piles. One pile will contain all the **long**-a words spelled **ai**. The other pile will have all the **long**-a words spelled **ay**.*
Step 2: Sort Have children sort the words. If you are doing a closed sort, model sorting one or two of the words. Then have children sort the remaining words. Circulate and ask children questions about why they are putting specific words into each category.	*Watch as I sort the first word: **gray**. Read the word with me: **gray**. In this word, the **long**-a sound is spelled **ay**, so I will put this in the "**ay**" pile.*
Step 3: Check and Discuss Review the words in each sort category. Ask children what they learned about these words from doing the sort. Guide children to the word-awareness aspect of each sort that will assist them in reading and writing. Have children store the word cards for future sorts (e.g., a timed sort using these words).	*What do you notice about these **long**-a spellings? Look at where each spelling appears in the words. (Provide time for children to discuss.) The **long**-a spelling **ai** never appears at the end of a word, but the **ay** spelling does. That is good to remember because it can help us spell new words with **long** a.* *For example, I want to spell the word **play**. Where do you hear the **long**-a sound—in the middle or at the end? That's right; it's at the end. So, will I spell the **long**-a sound in **play** with the letters **ai**? No. Why? Because that spelling doesn't appear at the end of a word. Which spelling should I use? That's right—**ay**. This spelling does appear at the end of words like **say, may, gray,** and **play**.*

Word Sorts: Kindergarten

Above Grade Level	On Grade Level	Below Grade Level
Target Skill: Short *a*		
at, cat, mat, sat, bat	at, cat, mat	at, cat
an, can, man, fan, pan	an, can, man	an, can
Target Skill: Short *i*		
it, sit, fit, pit, bit	it, sit, fit	it, sit
in, pin, fin, tin, bin	in, pin, fin	in, pin
Target Skill: Short *o*		
mop, hop, top, pop, plop	mop, hop, top, pop	mop, hop
not, hot, lot, pot, plot	not, hot, lot, pot	not, hot
Target Skill: Short *u*		
fun, sun, bun, run, rush	fun, sun, run, bun	fun, sun, run
nut, cut, hut, but, shut	nut, cut, hut, but	nut, cut, hut
Target Skill: Short *e*		
red, bed, fed, led, sled, shed	red, bed, fed, led, Ted	red, bed, fed
sell, tell, bell, fell, spell, shell	sell, tell, bell, fell, well	sell, tell, bell

Section 5
Word-Sort Sets

Word Sorts: Grade 1

Word Sorts: Grade 1

Above Grade Level	On Grade Level	Below Grade Level
Target Skill: Short *a*		
hat, bat, can, pan, had, bad	hat, bat, can, pan, had, bad	hat, bat, can, pan, had, bad
that, chat, plan, than, glad, Brad	mat, cat, man, ran, mad, sad	
Target Skill: Short *i*		
sit, fit, will, fill, sick, pick	sit, fit, will, fill, sick, pick	sit, fit, will, fill, sick, pick
quit, skit, spill, chill, stick, quick	hit, kit, bill, hill, lick, kick	
Target Skill: Short *o*		
top, hop, not, hot, sock, lock	top, hop, not, hot, sock, lock	top, hop, not, hot, sock, lock
chop, drop, shot, spot, clock, shock	mop, pop, pot, lot, rock, dock	
Target Skill: Short *u*		
cub, rub, cut, nut, luck, duck	cub, rub, cut, nut, luck, duck	cub, rub, cut, nut, luck, duck
club, scrub, shut, strut, stuck, truck	sub, tub, but, hut, tuck, puck	
Target Skill: Short *e*		
men, ten, led, bed, bell, tell	men, ten, led, bed, bell, tell	men, ten, led, bed, bell, tell
then, when, sled, shed, spell, smell	hen, pen, fed, red, well, sell	
Target Skill: Consonant Blends (*l*-blends)		
black, block, plant, play, sled, slip	black, block, plant, play, sled, slip	black, block, plant, play, sled, slip
glide, globe, flame, float, close, cloud	glad, glass, flag, flop, class, cliff	lack, lock, pant, pay, led, lip

Word Sorts: Grade 1

Section 5
Word-Sort Sets

Above Grade Level	On Grade Level	Below Grade Level
Target Skill: Consonant Blends (s-blends)		
smell, smog, snack, snug, skin, skit	smell, smog, snack, snug, skin, skit	smell, snack, stop, spot, skit
swimming, swelling, stopping, stepping spelling, spotting	swim, swell, stop, step, spell, spot	sell, sack, top, pot, kit
Target Skill: Consonant Blends (r-blends)		
frog, from, grab, grass, trip, truck	frog, from, grab, grass, trip, truck	frog, trip, truck, crab, drip
bringing, brushing, crashing, crossing, dripping, dressing	brick, bring, crab, crash, drip, dress	fog, rip, tuck, cab, dip
Target Skill: Digraph sh		
shop, ship, fish, wish, cash	shop, ship, fish, wish, cash	shop, ship, fish, wish, cash
shake, shoe, splash, dishes, pushes	shut, shell, fresh, crush, trash	hop, hip, fit, will, cat
Target Skill: Digraph th		
thin, thick, with, math, bath	thin, thick, with, math, bath	thin, thick, with, math, bath
thumb, three, both, teeth, fifth	thing, think, moth, Beth, path	tin, tick, wit, mat, bat
Target Skill: Digraph ch and Trigraph tch		
chip, chop, match, pitch, bench	chip, chop, match, pitch, bench	chip, chop, match, pitch, bench
chair, cheese, child, branches, scratches	chat, chin, path, witch, bunch	hip, hop, mat, pit, bent
Target Skill: Digraph wh		
what, where, when, why, which	what, where, when, why, which	what, when, which
window, wagon, water, wash, work	win, wig, will, wet, web	win, will, wet
Target Skill: Digraph ng and Blend nk		
sing, ring, king, pink, sink	sing, ring, king, pink, sink	sing, ring, king, pink, sink, drink
singing, ringing, thinking,* drinking,* thanking*	swing, thing, drink, thank, trunk	

* Will appear in multiple sort columns

Section 5
Word-Sort Sets

Word Sorts: Grade 1

Above Grade Level	On Grade Level	Below Grade Level
Target Skill: Final e		
tape, hate, bite, ride, hope, note	tape, hate, bite, ride, hope, note	tape, hate, bite, ride, hope, note
milkshake, shave, invite, drive, telephone, those	bake, gave, kite, five, home, vote	tap, hat, bit, rid, hop, not
Target Skill: Long a		
rain, train, paint, play, stay	rain, train, paint, play, stay	rain, train, paint, play, stay
unpaid, unafraid, remain, repay, subway	brain, nail, pail, gray, way	ran, plan, trap, pan, stack
Target Skill: Long e		
read, team, keep, week, seed	read, team, keep, week, seed	read, team, keep, week, seed
unreal, unclear, sixteen, oversleep, agreed	beach, clean, dream, three, sleep	red, bed, let, met, ten
Target Skill: Long o		
boat, coat, goat, row, grow	boat, coat, goat, row, grow	boat, coat, goat, row, grow
raincoat, rowboat, railroad, rainbow, below	toast, coast, show, slow, snow	box, top, mop, got, hot
Target Skill: Long i		
light, night, high, my, try	light, night, high, my, try	light, night, high, my, try
midnight, sunlight, butterfly, July, reply	bright, flight, sky, shy, why	six, big, fit, zip, will
Target Skill: Long u		
cute, use, huge, few, menu	cute, use, huge, few, menu	cute, use, huge, few, menu
rescue, argue, continue, usual, museum	cube, mule, unit, human, music	cut, us, hug, but, bug

Word Sorts: Grade 1

Section 5
Word-Sort Sets

Above Grade Level	On Grade Level	Below Grade Level
Target Skill: *r*-Controlled Vowels *er, ir, ur*		
girl, bird, verb, fern, burn, hurt	girl, bird, verb, fern, burn, hurt	girl, bird, verb, fern, burn, hurt
squirting, twirling, concern, observe, disturb, sunburn	stir, third, never, letter, nurse, purse	lip, bid, vet, fed, bun, hut
Target Skill: *r*-Controlled Vowel *ar*		
far, car, hard, yard, cart, part	far, car, hard, yard, cart, part	far, car, hard, yard, cart, part
superstar, guitar, barnyard, discard, apart, restart	jar, scar, card, guard, chart, smart	fan, can, had, mad, cat, pat
Target Skill: *r*-Controlled Vowels *or, ore, oor*		
more, store, born, corn, door, floor	more, store, born, corn, door, floor	more, store, born, corn, door, floor
explore, anymore, popcorn, unicorn, outdoor, indoor	score, shore, thorn, morning	mop, stop, box, fox
Target Skill: *r*-Controlled Vowels *air, ear, ere, are*		
hair, chair, bear, tear, where, there, care, share	hair, chair, bear, tear, where, there, care, share	hair, chair, bear, tear, where, there, care, share
repair, unfair, wearing, underwear, prepare, beware	fair, stair, pear, wear, square, rare	
Target Skill: Diphthong *oi/oy*		
boy, joy, oil, boil, coin	boy, joy, oil, boil, coin	boy, joy, oil, boil, coin, join
cowboy, enjoy, spoiled, broiled, rejoin, joined	toy, soy, soil, broil, join	

Word Sorts: Grade 1

Section 5 — Word-Sort Sets

Above Grade Level	On Grade Level	Below Grade Level
Target Skill: Diphthong ou/ow		
out, shout, found, mouth, down, clown	out, shout, found, mouth, down, clown	out, shout, found, sound, mouth, south, down, clown
about, throughout, around, south, touchdown, downtown	about, round, sound, south, brown, clown	
Target Skill: Complex Vowel /ô/ a, aw		
fall, small, walk, talk, jaw, saw	fall, small, walk, talk, jaw, saw	fall, small, walk, talk, jaw, saw
baseball, football, sidewalk, beanstalk, jigsaw, withdraw	tall, mall, chalk, stalk, straw, draw	
Target Skill: Short oo		
good, wood, book, cook, could	good, wood, book, cook, could	good, wood, book, cook, could, would
redwood, understood, overlook, notebook, shouldn't	hood, stood, took, shook, would	
Target Skill: Long oo (oo, ew, ue, u_e)		
new, blew, blue, glue, tooth, room, June, tune	new, blew, blue, glue, tooth, room, June, tune	new, blew, blue, glue, tooth, room, June, tune
threw, outgrew, untrue, avenue, balloon, seafood, include, costume	grew, chew, clue, true, broom, moon, tube, rule	

Word Sorts (With Multisyllabic Words): Grade 2

Section 5
Word-Sort Sets

Above Grade Level	On Grade Level	Below Grade Level
Target Skill: Consonant Blends (3-letter and complex blends)		
scrap, scratch, scream, scramble, square, squeak, squeeze, squirrel, string, strip, stretch strawberry, spring, spray, spread, sprinkle, splash, splendid, splinter	scrap, scratch, scream, square, squeak, squeeze string, strip, stretch, spring, spray, spread	scrap, scratch, square, squeak, string, strip, spring, spray glad, glass, flag, flop, class, cliff
Target Skill: Digraph *sh*		
shake, shoe, splash, dishes, pushes shoulder, shampoo, shoelace, brushes, smashing	shop, ship, fish, wish, cash shake, shoe, splash, dishes, pushes	shop, ship, fish, wish, cash shut, shell, fresh, crush, trash
Target Skill: Digraph *th*		
thumb, three, both, teeth, fifth thermometer, Thanksgiving, thousand, length, strength	thin, thick, with, math, bath thumb, three, both, teeth, fifth	thin, thick, with, math, bath thing, think, moth, Beth, path
Target Skill: Digraph *ch* and Trigraph *tch*		
chair, cheese, child, branches, scratches cheeseburger, children, chocolate, sandwich, search	chip, chop, match, pitch, bench chair, cheese, child, branches, scratches	chip, chop, match, pitch, bench chat, chin, patch, witch, bunch
Target Skill: Digraph *wh*		
window, wagon, water, wash, work whisper, wheelbarrow, wheelchair, whatever, whisker	what, where, when, why, which window, wagon, water, wash, work	what, where, when, why, which win, wig, will, wet, web

Word Sorts: Grade 2

Section 5 — Word-Sort Sets

Above Grade Level	On Grade Level	Below Grade Level
Target Skill: Digraph *ng* and Blend *nk*		
singing, ringing, thinking,* drinking,* thanking*	sing, ring, king, pink, sink	sing, ring, king, pink, sink
strength, hunger, youngest, shrunk, thankfully	singing, ringing, thinking,* drinking,* thanking*	swing, thing, drink, thank, trunk
Target Skill: Final *e*		
milkshake, shave, invite, drive, telephone, those	tape, hate, bite, ride, hope, note	tape, hate, bite, ride, hope, note
(exceptions) advantage, climate, determine, magazine, purpose, improve	milkshake, shave, invite, drive, telephone, those	bake, gave, kite, five, home, vote
Target Skill: Long *a*		
unpaid, unafraid, remain, repay, subway	rain, train, paint, play, stay	rain, train, paint, play, stay
mermaid, terrain, yesterday, holiday	unpaid, unafraid, remain, repay, subway	brain, nail, pail, gray, way
Target Skill: Long *e*		
unreal, unclear, sixteen, oversleep, agreed	read, team, keep, week, seed	read, team, keep, week, seed
disappear, mistreat, misread, disagree, fourteen	unreal, unclear, sixteen, oversleep, agreed	beach, clean, dream, three, sleep
Target Skill: Long *o*		
raincoat, rowboat, railroad, rainbow, below	boat, coat, goat, row, grow	boat, coat, goat, row, grow
unload, workload, afloat, unknown, windblown	raincoat, rowboat, railroad, rainbow, below	toast, coast, show, slow, snow
Target Skill: Long *i*		
midnight, sunlight, butterfly, July, reply	light, night, high, my, try	light, night, high, my, try
stoplight, eyesight, supply, identify, occupy	midnight, sunlight, butterfly, July, reply	bright, flight, sky, shy, why

* Will appear in multiple sort columns

Word Sorts: Grade 2

Section 5
Word-Sort Sets

Above Grade Level	On Grade Level	Below Grade Level
Target Skill: Long u		
rescue, argue, continue, usual, museum	cute, use, huge, few, menu	cute, use, huge, few, menu
review, preview, continue, value, uniform,	rescue, argue, continue, usual, museum	cube, mule, unit, human, music
Target Skill: r-Controlled Vowels er, ir, ur		
squirting, twirling, concern, observe, disturb, sunburn	girl, bird, verb, fern, burn, hurt	girl, bird, verb, fern, burn, hurt
superb, submerge, deserve, blackbird, nocturnal, purge	squirting, twirling, concern, observe, disturb, sunburn	stir, third, never, letter, nurse, purse
Target Skill: r-Controlled Vowel ar		
superstar, guitar, barnyard, discard, apart, restart	far, car, hard, yard, cart, part	far, car, hard, yard, cart, part
bizarre, jaguar, postcard, departed, outsmarted, lifeguard	superstar, guitar, barnyard, discard, apart, restart	jar, scar, card, guard, chart, smart
Target Skill: r-Controlled Vowels or, ore, oor		
explore, anymore, popcorn, unicorn, outdoor, indoor	more, store, born, corn, door, floor	more, store, born, corn, door, floor
therefore, ignore, acorn, support, transport, export	explore, anymore, popcorn, unicorn, outdoor, indoor	score, shore, thorn, morning
Target Skill: r-Controlled Vowels air, ear, ere, are		
repair, unfair, wearing, underwear, prepare, beware	hair, chair, bear, tear, where, there, care, share	hair, chair, bear, tear, where, there, care, share
upstairs, millionaire, nightmare, unaware, compare	repair, unfair, wearing, underwear, prepare, beware	fair, stair, pear, wear, square, rare

Section 5
Word-Sort Sets

Word Sorts: Grade 2

Above Grade Level	On Grade Level	Below Grade Level
Target Skill: Diphthong *oi/oy*		
cowboy, enjoy, spoiled, broiled, rejoin, joined enjoyable, destroy, annoyed, viewpoint, disappoint	boy, joy, oil, boil, coin cowboy, enjoy, spoiled, broiled, rejoin, joined	boy, joy, oil, boil, coin toy, soy, soil, broil, join
Target Skill: Diphthong *ou/ow*		
about, throughout, around, south, touchdown, downtown without, cookout, doghouse, firehouse, background, campground	out, shout, found, mouth, down, clown about, throughout, around, south, touchdown, downtown	out, shout, found, mouth, down, clown about, round, sound, south, brown, crown
Target Skill: Complex Vowel /ô/ *a, au, aw*		
baseball, football, sidewalk, beanstalk, jigsaw, withdraw waterfall, basketball, crosswalk, taught, caught	fall, small, walk, talk, jaw, saw baseball, football, sidewalk, beanstalk, jigsaw, withdraw	fall, small, walk, talk, jaw, saw tall, mall, chalk, stalk, straw, draw
Target Skill: Short *oo*		
redwood, understood, overlook, notebook, shouldn't neighborhood, misunderstood, barefoot, underfoot, wouldn't	good, wood, book, cook, could redwood, understood, overlook, notebook, shouldn't	good, wood, book, cook, could hood, stood, took, shook, would
Target Skill: Long *oo* (*oo, ew, ue, u_e, ou*)		
threw, outgrew, untrue, avenue, balloon, seafood, include, costume soup, group, pollute, salute, pursue	new, blew, blue, glue, tooth, room, June, tune threw, outgrew, untrue, avenue, balloon, seafood, include, costume	new, blew, blue, glue, tooth, room, June, tune grew, chew, clue, true, broom, moon, tube, rule
Target Skill: Silent Letters		
write, wrist, know, knob, sign, gnat written, knowledge, assign, doubt, climber	write, wrist, know, knob, sign, gnat wrong, wren, knife, knee, knock	write, wrist, know, knob, sign, gnat

Word Sorts: Grade 2

Section 5
Word-Sort Sets

Above Grade Level	On Grade Level	Below Grade Level
Target Skill: Prefixes *un-*, *re-*		
unwrap, unhurt, unlock, reheat, reread	unwrap, unhurt, unlock, reheat, reread	unwrap, unhurt, unlock, reheat, reread
unlikely, unafraid, rebuilding, reappear, replacing	unclear, unpack, rebuild, retie, rewrite	wrap, hurt, lock, heat, read
Target Skill: Suffix *-ing*		
stepping, skipping, floating, matching, jumping	spelling, playing, stopping, painting, helping	spelling, playing, stopping, painting, helping
stopping, repainting, replanting, reteaching, unboxing	stepping, skipping, floating, matching, jumping	spell, play, stop, paint, help
Target Skill: Suffix *-ed*		
jogged, closed, lasted, melted, fixed, stopped	grabbed, shaved, ended, planted, asked, helped	grabbed, shaved, ended, planted, asked, helped
rhymed, phoned, guided, hinted, dropped, guessed	jogged, closed, lasted, melted, fixed, stopped	grab, shave, end, plant, ask, help
Target Skill: Suffixes *-y*, *-ly*		
crazy, easy, calmly, likely, nicely	hairy, jumpy, mostly, yearly, weekly	hairy, jumpy, mostly, yearly, weekly
bouncy, glittery, gloomy, generally, friendly	crazy, easy, calmly, likely, nicely	hair, jump, most, year, week
Target Skill: Compound Words		
airplane, airsick, football, footprint, snowball, snowstorm	airplane, backpack, bathroom, footprint, snowball	airplane, backpack, bathroom, footprint, snowball
seashell, seafood, everywhere, everything, headache, headphones	airsick, bedroom, football, backseat, snowstorm	plane, pack, room, foot, snow
Target Skill: Final Stable Syllables (*tion*, *sion*, *ture*, *sure*)		
addition, vacation, erosion, explosion, measure, treasure, picture, mixture	direction, pressure, confusion, nature	action, question, vision, confusion, measure, treasure, picture, mixture
celebration, definition, television, invasion, pleasure, exposure, texture, moisture	addition, vacation, erosion, vision, measure, treasure, picture, mixture	

Section 5: Word-Sort Sets

Word Sorts: Grade 2

Section 5 — Word-Sort Sets

Above Grade Level	On Grade Level	Below Grade Level
Target Skill: Closed Syllables		
napkin, cabin, dentist, insect, mitten	napkin, cabin, dentist, insect, mitten	napkin, dentist, mitten
commonly, unhidden, insulted, magnetic, publishing	nap, cab, den, in, mitt	nap, den, mitt
Target Skill: Open Syllables		
crazy, bonus, pilot, female, music	bacon, frozen, silent, even, pupil	bacon, frozen, silent, even, pupil
location, donation, secretly, recently, prefixes	crazy, bonus, pilot, female, music	we, go, hi, she, so
Target Skill: r-Controlled Vowel Syllables		
market, dirty, perfect, forty, number	market, dirty, perfect, forty, number	market, dirty, perfect, forty, number
suburban, absorbing, discarded, expertly, flavorful	person, barber, birthday, doctor, slipper	mark, dirt, purr, four, burn
Target Skill: Vowel-Team Syllables		
railroad, raincoat, seaweed, highway, oatmeal	railroad, raincoat, seaweed, highway, oatmeal	railroad, raincoat, seaweed, highway, oatmeal
explaining, repeated, annoying, complaining, proceeded	freedom, explain, mermaid, repeat, window	road, rain, sea, high, oats
Target Skill: Consonant + le Syllables		
curable, scramble, brittle, gentle, tricycle, vehicle, puzzle, fizzle, purple, sample, eagle, bugle, hurdle, riddle, pickle, freckle	table, bubble, little, turtle, circle, uncle, puzzle, fizzle, purple, simple, eagle, bugle, handle, riddle, pickle, buckle	table, little, circle, puzzle, purple
		bubble, turtle, uncle, fizzle, simple
Target Skill: Final-e Syllables		
invite, complete, delete, reptile, expose	hopeless, lifetime, sidewalk, unmade, female	hopeless, lifetime, sidewalk, unmade, female
advice, describe, dispose, invade, locate	invite, complete, delete, reptile, expose	hope, time, side, made, male

SECTION 6

Word-Building Center

Every phonics lesson should include encoding (spelling/writing) activities for children to engage in every day. It takes longer to transfer these patterns to writing than reading. Encoding activities can vary, each with an important instructional focus. One such activity is word building, in which children use letter cards or magnetic letters to manipulate sounds and spellings in a series of words.

The word-building activities in this section offer joyful learning alternative activities to build spelling proficiency. They can also be made into highly engaging and purposeful learning centers. If you want to reuse these activity sheets, place them in a clear plastic folder and have children use dry-erase markers to complete them. Once completed and checked (create a self-checking card), the sheets can be wiped off and reused.

Materials Needed	The following pages provide templates for fun activities that build spelling proficiency. These templates can be used for whole- and small-group activities, learning centers, and at-home engagement. • Pages 144–166 feature word-building spinners. • Pages 167–169 provide word-building letter cubes. • Pages 170–191 present build-a-word houses. • Pages 192–212 feature "what's my word?" activities that also help build vocabulary. • Pages 213–215 provide word-ladder templates. • Page 216 offers additional fun activities for the whole class, small groups, and individual students.
Length of Activity	5–10 minutes
Location	school or home

Principle 4: Daily Spelling and Writing Activities

Skills Practiced

Phonemic Awareness ☐

Handwriting ☐

Spelling ☑

Decoding ☑

Dictation ☐

Writing ☐

Section 6 downloadables are available here.

Section 6
Word-Building Center

Activity 1: Spin-a-Word

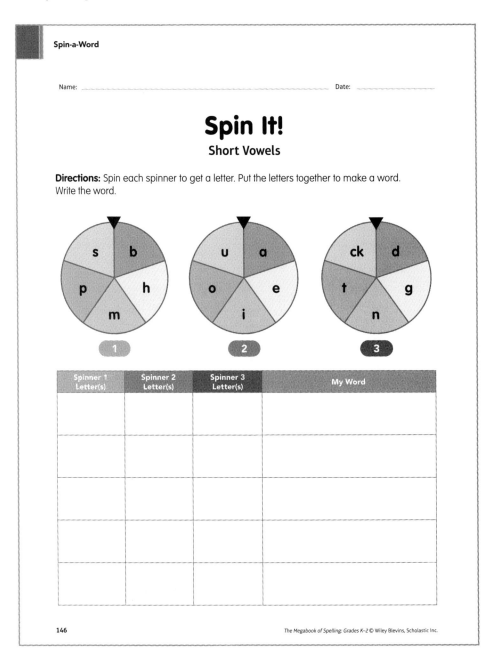

To the teacher: This is a sample spinner. Spinner pages are created for multiple skills. In addition, a blank template is provided on the next page for you to create your own Spin-a-Word spinners. To use a spinner, have a child place a paper clip on the spinner and use a sharpened pencil to hold one end of the paper clip in place. The child then flicks a finger to make the paper clip spin.

Spin-a-Word

Name: _____ Date: _____

Spin It!

Skill: _____

Directions: Spin each spinner to get a letter. Put the letters together to make a word. Write the word.

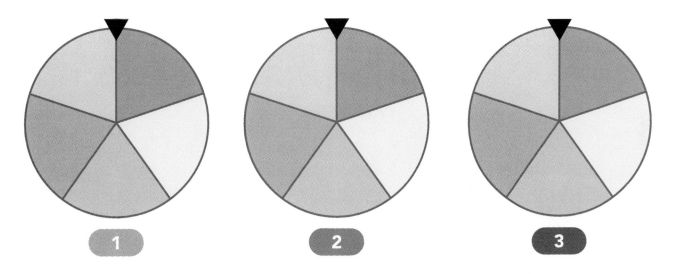

Spinner 1 Letter(s)	Spinner 2 Letter(s)	Spinner 3 Letter(s)	My Word

The Megabook of Spelling: Grades K–2 © Wiley Blevins, Scholastic Inc.

Spin-a-Word

Name: _____ Date: _____

Spin It!
Short Vowels

Directions: Spin each spinner to get a letter. Put the letters together to make a word. Write the word.

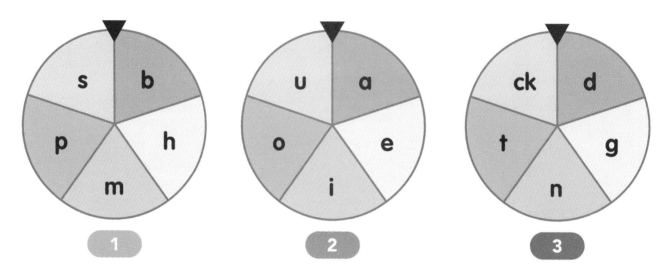

Spinner 1 Letter(s)	Spinner 2 Letter(s)	Spinner 3 Letter(s)	My Word

146 The Megabook of Spelling: Grades K–2 © Wiley Blevins, Scholastic Inc.

Spin-a-Word

Name: _____   Date: _____

Spin It!
Short Vowels with Blends

Directions: Spin each spinner to get a letter. Put the letters together to make a word. Write the word.

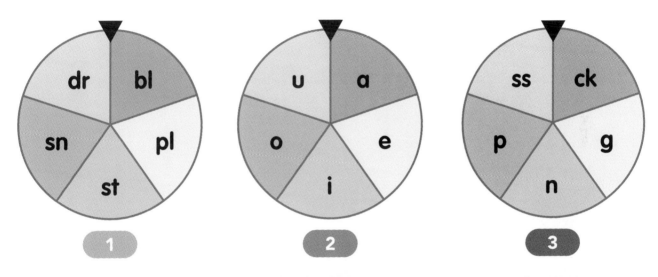

Spinner 1 Letter(s)	Spinner 2 Letter(s)	Spinner 3 Letter(s)	My Word

The Megabook of Spelling: Grades K–2 © Wiley Blevins, Scholastic Inc.

Spin-a-Word

Name: _____   Date: _____

Spin It!
Short Vowels with Digraphs

Directions: Spin each spinner to get a letter. Put the letters together to make a word. Write the word.

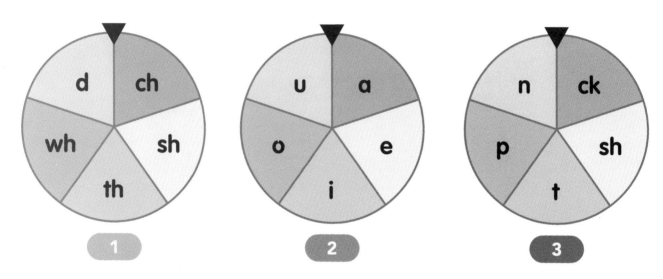

Spinner 1 Letter(s)	Spinner 2 Letter(s)	Spinner 3 Letter(s)	My Word

Spin-a-Word

Name: _____ Date: _____

Spin It!
Final e

Directions: Spin each spinner to get a letter. Put the letters together to make a word. Write the word.

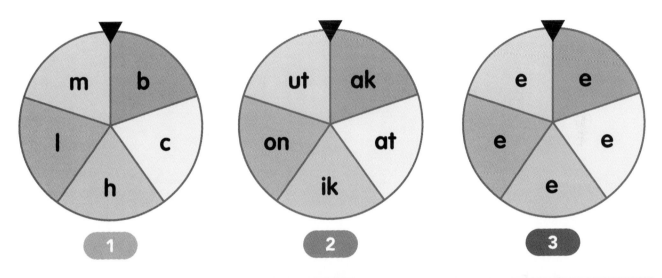

Spinner 1 Letter(s)	Spinner 2 Letter(s)	Spinner 3 Letter(s)	My Word

149

Spin-a-Word

Name: _____ Date: _____

Spin It!
Long *a*

Directions: Spin each spinner to get a letter. Put the letters together to make a word. Write the word.

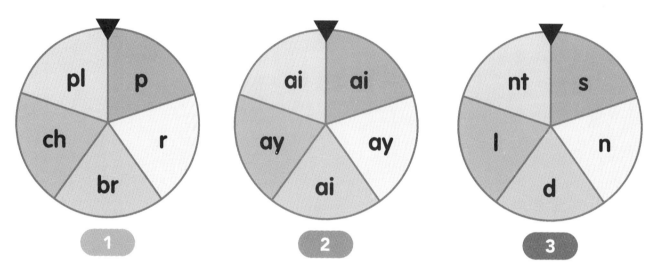

Spinner 1 Letter(s)	Spinner 2 Letter(s)	Spinner 3 Letter(s)	My Word

Spin-a-Word

Name: _____ Date: _____

Spin It!
Long e

Directions: Spin each spinner to get a letter. Put the letters together to make a word. Write the word.

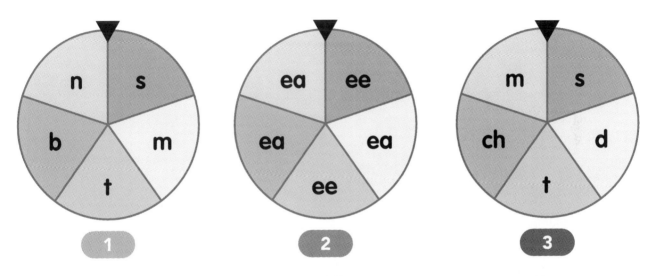

Spinner 1 Letter(s)	Spinner 2 Letter(s)	Spinner 3 Letter(s)	My Word

The Megabook of Spelling: Grades K–2 © Wiley Blevins, Scholastic Inc.

Spin-a-Word

Name: _____ Date: _____

Spin It!
Long *i*

Directions: Spin each spinner to get a letter. Put the letters together to make a word. Write the word.

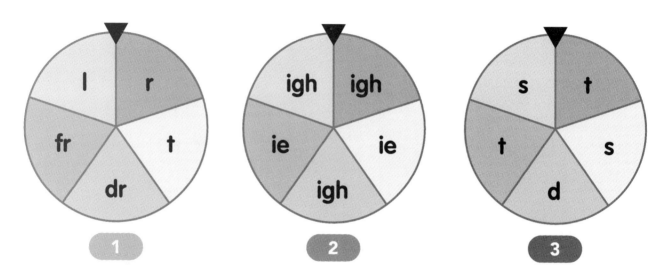

Spinner 1 Letter(s)	Spinner 2 Letter(s)	Spinner 3 Letter(s)	My Word

Spin-a-Word

Name: _____ Date: _____

Spin It!
Long *o*

Directions: Spin each spinner to get a letter. Put the letters together to make a word. Write the word.

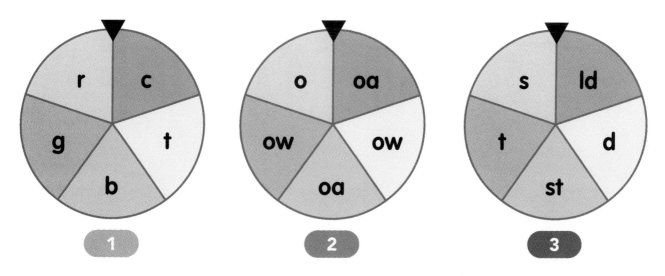

Spinner 1 Letter(s)	Spinner 2 Letter(s)	Spinner 3 Letter(s)	My Word

The Megabook of Spelling: Grades K–2 © Wiley Blevins, Scholastic Inc.

Spin-a-Word

Name: _____   Date: _____

Spin It!
Diphthongs *oi, oy*

Directions: Spin each spinner to get a letter. Put the letters together to make a word. Write the word.

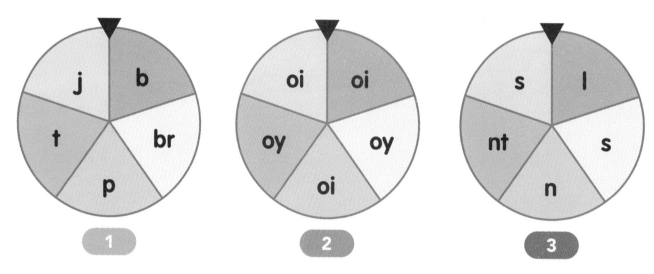

Spinner 1 Letter(s)	Spinner 2 Letter(s)	Spinner 3 Letter(s)	My Word

Spin-a-Word

Name: _____ Date: _____

Spin It!

Diphthongs *ou, ow*

Directions: Spin each spinner to get a letter. Put the letters together to make a word. Write the word.

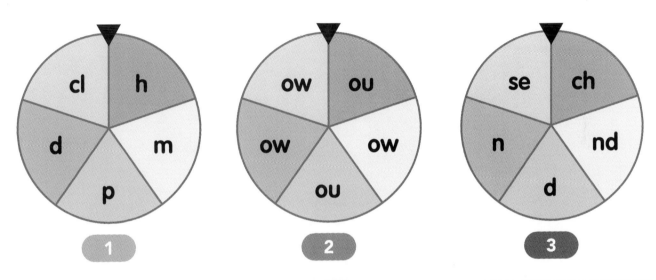

Spinner 1 Letter(s)	Spinner 2 Letter(s)	Spinner 3 Letter(s)	My Word

The Megabook of Spelling: Grades K–2 © Wiley Blevins, Scholastic Inc.

Spin-a-Word

Name: _____ Date: _____

Spin It!
r-Controlled Vowel *ar*

Directions: Spin each spinner to get a letter. Put the letters together to make a word. Write the word.

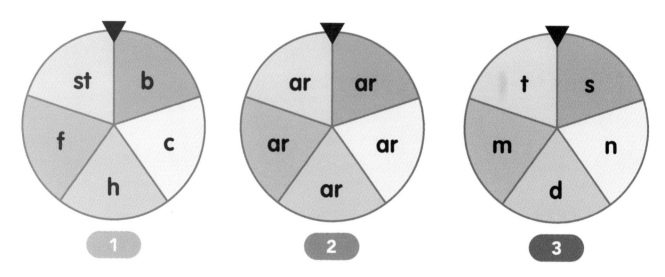

Spinner 1 Letter(s)	Spinner 2 Letter(s)	Spinner 3 Letter(s)	My Word

Spin-a-Word

Name: _____ Date: _____

Spin It!
r-Controlled Vowel *or*

Directions: Spin each spinner to get a letter. Put the letters together to make a word. Write the word.

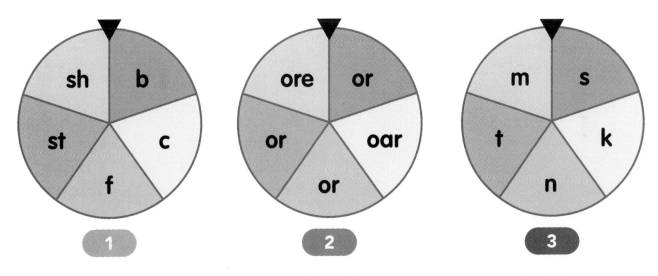

Spinner 1 Letter(s)	Spinner 2 Letter(s)	Spinner 3 Letter(s)	My Word

The Megabook of Spelling: Grades K–2 © Wiley Blevins, Scholastic Inc.

Spin-a-Word

Name: _____   Date: _____

Spin It!
r-Controlled Vowels er, ir, ur

Directions: Spin each spinner to get a letter. Put the letters together to make a word. Write the word.

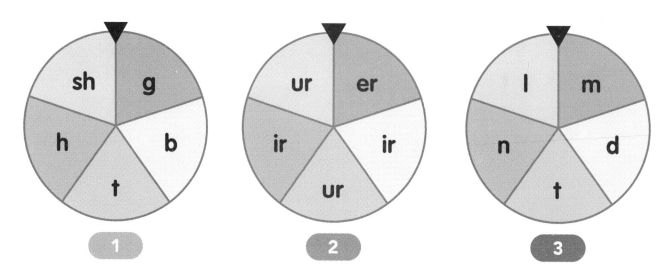

Spinner 1 Letter(s)	Spinner 2 Letter(s)	Spinner 3 Letter(s)	My Word

Spin-a-Word

Name: _____   Date: _____

Spin It!
Complex Vowel /ô/

Directions: Spin each spinner to get a letter. Put the letters together to make a word. Write the word.

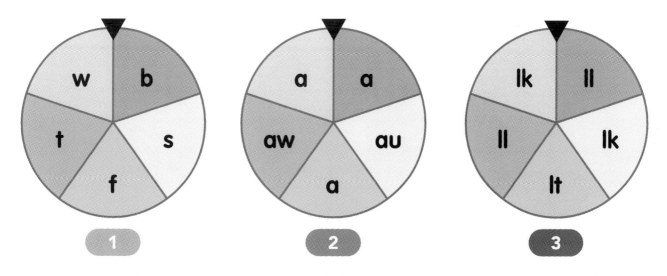

Spinner 1 Letter(s)	Spinner 2 Letter(s)	Spinner 3 Letter(s)	My Word

Spin-a-Word

Name: _____ Date: _____

Spin It!
Long *oo*

Directions: Spin each spinner to get a letter. Put the letters together to make a word. Write the word.

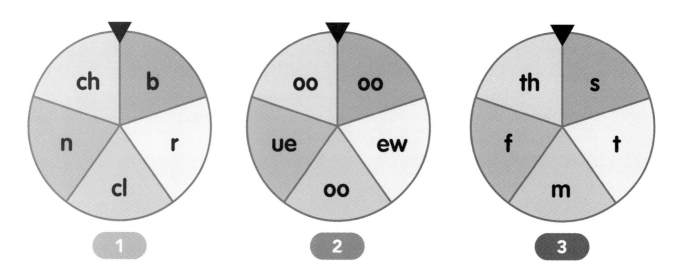

Spinner 1 Letter(s)	Spinner 2 Letter(s)	Spinner 3 Letter(s)	My Word

Spin-a-Word

Name: _____ Date: _____

Spin It!
Short oo

Directions: Spin each spinner to get a letter. Put the letters together to make a word. Write the word.

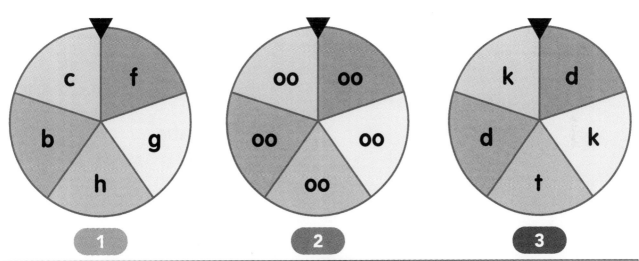

Spinner 1 Letter(s)	Spinner 2 Letter(s)	Spinner 3 Letter(s)	My Word

The Megabook of Spelling: Grades K–2 © Wiley Blevins, Scholastic Inc.

Spin-a-Word

Name: _____ Date: _____

Spin It!
Prefixes un-, re-, dis-

Directions: Spin each spinner to get a prefix and a word. Put them together to make a new word. Write the word.

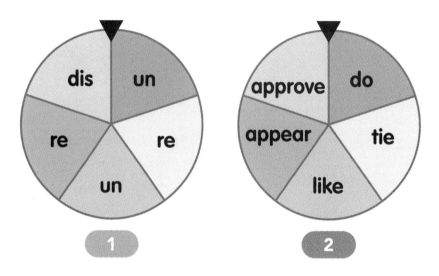

Spinner 1 Prefix	Spinner 2 Word	My Word

Spin-a-Word

Name: _____ Date: _____

Spin It!
Suffixes -s, -ing, -ed

Directions: Spin each spinner to get a word and a suffix. Put them together to make a new word. Write the word.

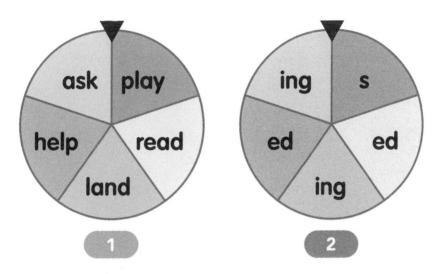

Spinner 1 Word	Spinner 2 Suffix	My Word

The Megabook of Spelling: Grades K–2 © Wiley Blevins, Scholastic Inc.

Spin It!
Suffixes -ful, -less

Directions: Spin each spinner to get a word and a suffix. Put them together to make a new word. Write the word.

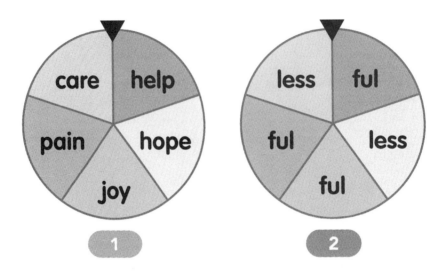

Spinner 1 Word	Spinner 2 Suffix	My Word

Spin-a-Word

Name: _____   Date: _____

Spin It!
Multisyllabic Words

Directions: Spin each spinner to get a syllable. Put the syllables together to make a word. Write the word.

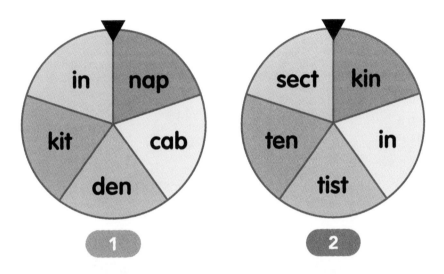

Spinner 1 Syllable	Spinner 2 Syllable	My Word

The Megabook of Spelling: Grades K–2 © Wiley Blevins, Scholastic Inc.

Spin-a-Word

Name: _____ Date: _____

Spin It!
Compound Words

Directions: Spin each spinner to get a word. Put the words together to make a compound word. Write the compound word.

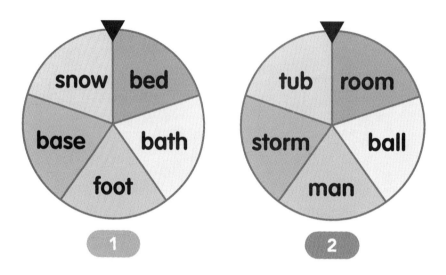

Spinner 1 Word	Spinner 2 Word	My Word

Activity 2: Letter Cubes

Roll-a-Word

(Players: 2 to 4)

Student Directions

1. Players take turns rolling all three cubes and reading the letters that land face up. The player then tries to use the letters to form words.

   • If one or more words can be formed, the player records the word(s) on a sheet of paper.

   • If not, the next player takes a turn.

2. Players continue taking turns. (Different players may form the same words.) The first player to form five different words wins the game.

Section 6
Word-Building Center

To the teacher: Copy and cut out the student directions above. Glue directions to the front of a ziplock bag. Copy the three letter cube patterns (pages 168–169) on card stock, cut them out, and assemble as shown below. Then place the cubes inside the bag. (A blank template is provided on page 169 for you to create your own letter cubes.)

Letter Cubes

To assemble each cube, cut and fold, as shown. Glue or tape closed.

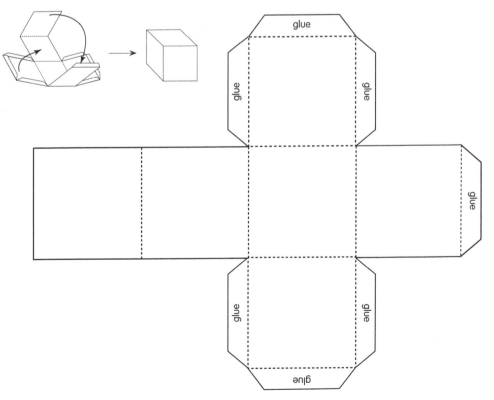

Letter Cubes

Cube 1 faces: tee, ba, ma, mo, pa, wi

Cube 2 faces: ing, em, ank, ink, ick, ree

Letter Cubes

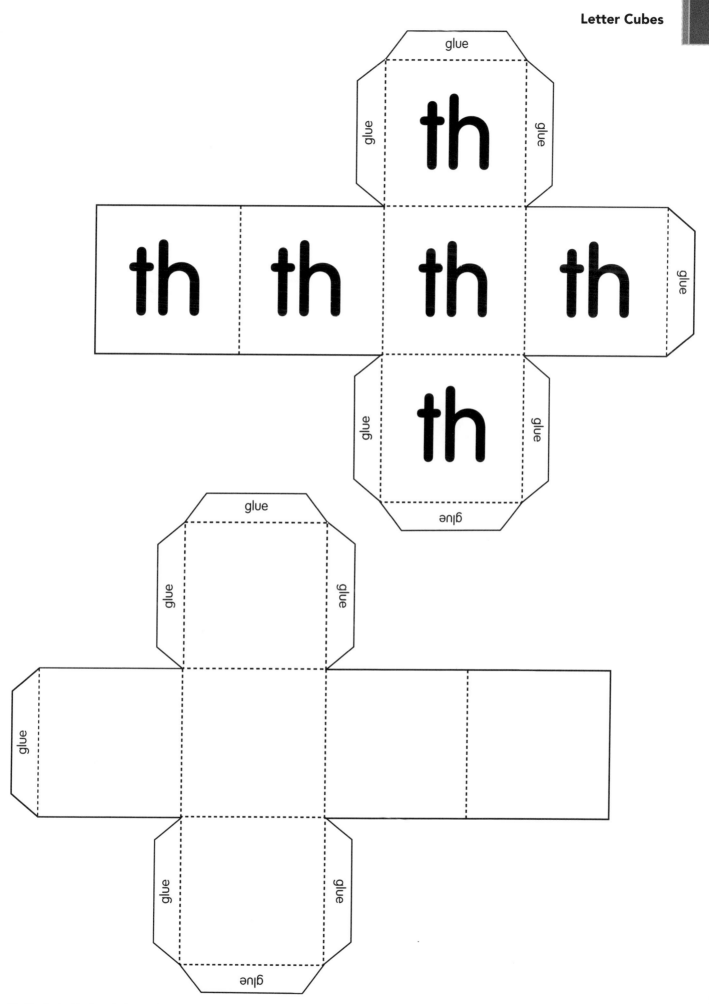

The Megabook of Spelling: Grades K–2 © Wiley Blevins, Scholastic Inc.

Section 6
Word-Building Center

Activity 3: Build-a-Word

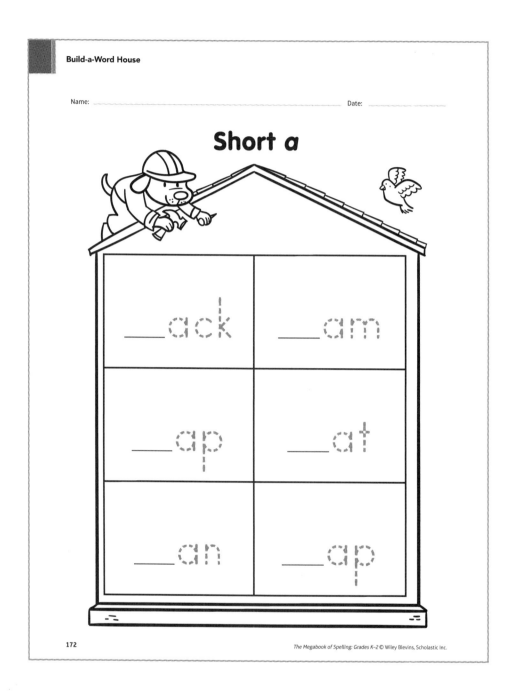

To the teacher: Have children write a consonant, blend, or digraph on the blank line to make a word, and then trace the gray spelling pattern (phonogram) to complete the word. Then have them read the words in their word houses to partners.

Build-a-Word House

Name: _____ Date: _____

Skill: _____

171

Build-a-Word House

Short a

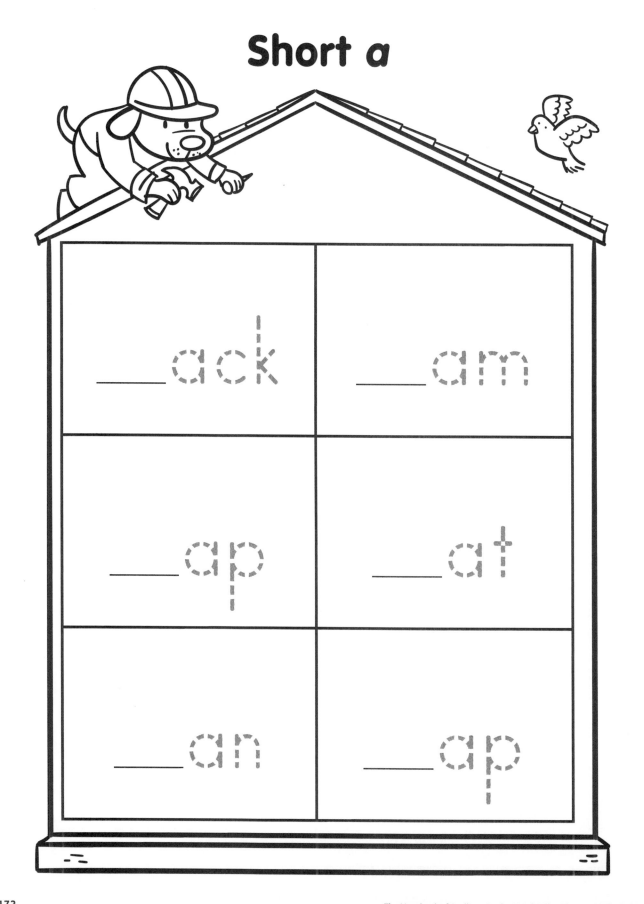

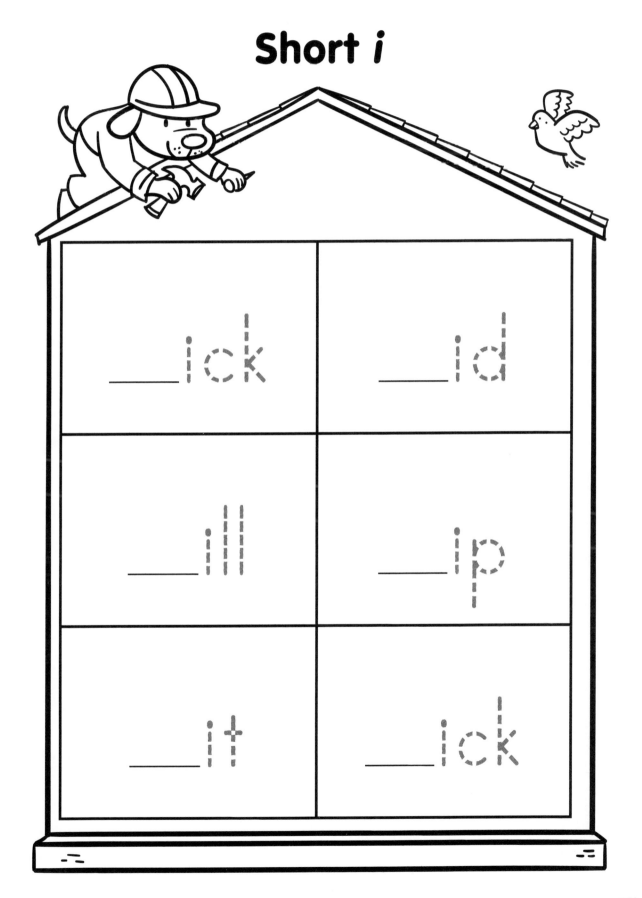

Build-a-Word House

Name: _____   Date: _____

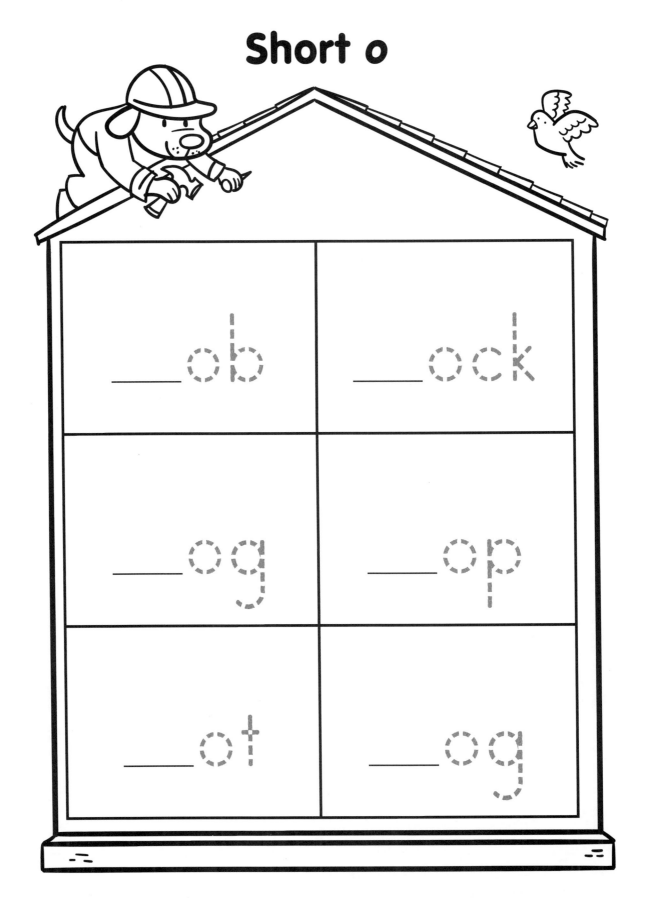

Build-a-Word House

Name: _____ Date: _____

Short u

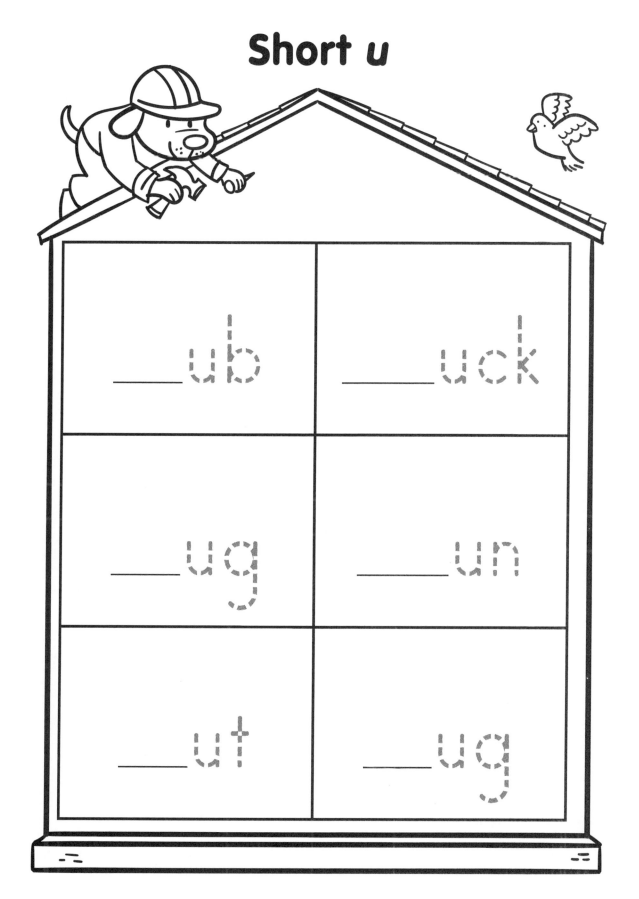

Build-a-Word House

Name: _____ Date: _____

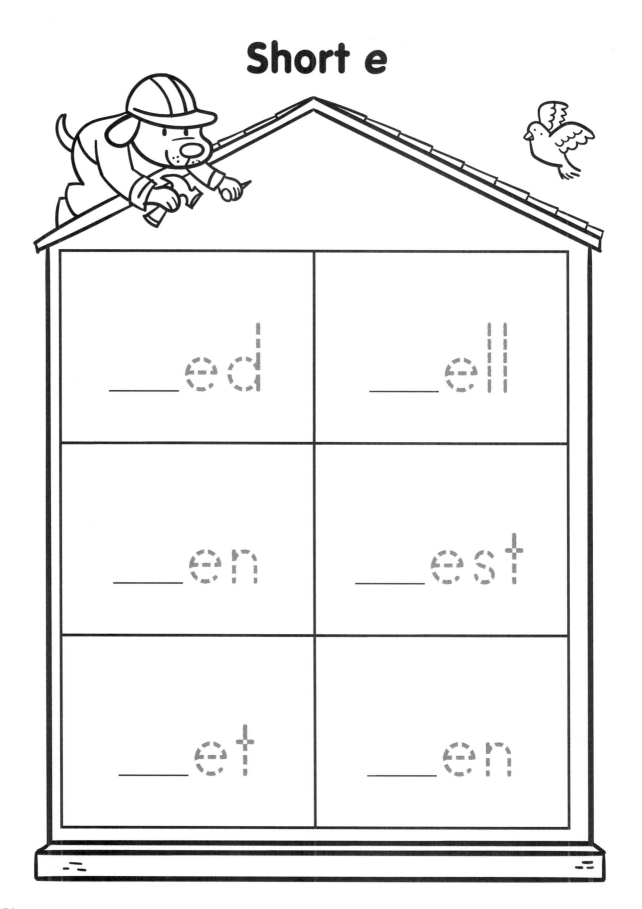

Build-a-Word House

Name: _____ Date: _____

Final e

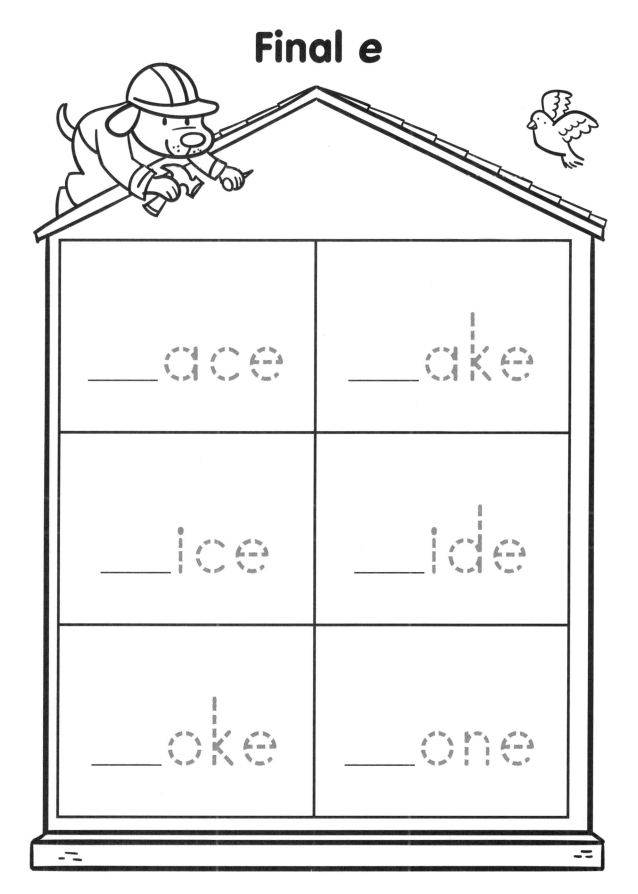

Build-a-Word House

Name: _____ Date: _____

Long a

__aid	__ail	__ain
__ay	__ey	__ail
__aid	__ain	__ay

Build-a-Word House

Name: _____ Date: _____

Long e

__each	__eak	__eam
__eat	__eed	__eep
__eet	__eep	__each

Build-a-Word House

Name: _____   Date: _____

Long o

__oat	__oe	__old
__oll	__ow	__own
__oat	__old	__ow

Build-a-Word House

Name: _____ Date: _____

Long i

___ie	___ied	___ies
___ight	___y	___ie
___ies	___ight	___y

The Megabook of Spelling: Grades K–2 © Wiley Blevins, Scholastic Inc.

Build-a-Word House

Name: _____ Date: _____

Long u

__u__e   __ew

__ue   __iew

u__e   __ue

Build-a-Word House

r-Controlled Vowels *er, ir, ur*

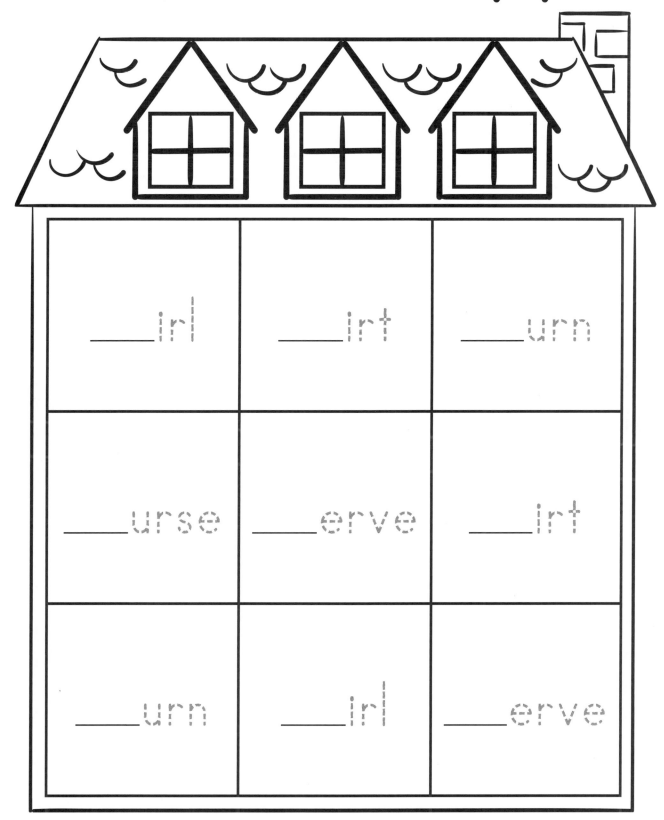

Build-a-Word House

Name: _____ Date: _____

Build-a-Word House

Name: _____ Date: _____

r-Controlled Vowels *or, ore, oar*

__oar	__ore	__ork
__orm	__orn	__ort
__ore	__ork	__orm

The Megabook of Spelling: Grades K–2 © Wiley Blevins, Scholastic Inc.   185

Build-a-Word House

Name: _____ Date: _____

r-Controlled Vowels
air, ear, ere, are

__air	__ear	__are
__ere	__air	__ear
__are	__ear	__are

Build-a-Word House

Name: _____ Date: _____

Diphthong *oi, oy*

Build-a-Word House

Name: _____ Date: _____

Diphthong *ou, ow*

_ouch	_ound	_ouse
_out	_ow	_owl
_own	_ouch	_out

Build-a-Word House

Complex Vowel /ô/ (a, au, aw)

Build-a-Word House

Name: _____ Date: _____

Short oo

___ood   ___ook   ___ould

___ull   ___ush   ___ook

___ood   ___ould   ___ull

Long oo (oo, ew, ue, u_e)

Section 6
Word-Building Center

Activity 4: Missing Letters (What's My Word?)

Missing Letters

Name: _____ Date: _____

What's My Word?
Consonant Blends

Directions: Read each clue. Look at the incomplete word. Write the missing letters to solve the clue.

1. The opposite of *go*.	_____ _____ op
2. You can drive this.	_____ _____ uck
3. A black-and-white animal that smells bad.	_____ _____ unk
4. This has stripes and stars.	_____ _____ ag
5. An animal that can hop.	_____ _____ og
⭐ 6. The season when it rains a lot.	_____ _____ _____ ing
⭐ 7. A mouse makes this sound.	_____ _____ _____ eak

194   *The Megabook of Spelling: Grades K–2* © Wiley Blevins, Scholastic Inc.

To the teacher: Have children read the clue for each word, and then fill in the missing letters or spelling pattern. Starred numbers feature more challenging words.

192   The Megabook of Spelling: Grades K–2

Missing Letters

Name: _____   Date: _____

What's My Word?
Short Vowels

Directions: Read each clue. Look at the incomplete word. Write the missing letters to solve the clue.

1.	This is a color.	r ____ d
2.	This is an animal.	c ____ t
3.	Not little.	b ____ g
4.	Not cold.	h ____ t
5.	When you have a good time, you have ____.	f ____ n
⭐ 6.	A dog or cat can be a ____.	p ____ t
⭐ 7.	Another word for *insect*.	b ____ g

The Megabook of Spelling: Grades K–2 © Wiley Blevins, Scholastic Inc.

Missing Letters

Name: _____ Date: _____

What's My Word?
Consonant Blends

Directions: Read each clue. Look at the incomplete word. Write the missing letters to solve the clue.

1. The opposite of *go*.	___ ___ op
2. You can drive this.	___ ___ uck
3. A black-and-white animal that smells bad.	___ ___ unk
4. This has stripes and stars.	___ ___ ag
5. An animal that can hop.	___ ___ og
6. ⭐ The season when it rains a lot.	___ ___ ___ ing
7. ⭐ A mouse makes this sound.	___ ___ ___ eak

Name: _____ Date: _____

What's My Word?
Consonant Digraphs

Directions: Read each clue. Look at the incomplete word. Write the missing letters to solve the clue.

1.	These are made from potatoes.	____ ____ ips
2.	This is a color.	____ ____ ite
3.	You do this when you add numbers.	ma ____ ____
4.	A big boat.	____ ____ ip
5.	You wear this on your finger.	ri ____ ____
⭐ 6.	This person flies on a broom.	wi ____ ____ ____
⭐ 7.	You eat this around noon each day.	lun ____ ____

The Megabook of Spelling: Grades K–2 © Wiley Blevins, Scholastic Inc.

Missing Letters

Name: _____ Date: _____

What's My Word?
Final *e*

Directions: Read each clue. Look at the incomplete word. Write the missing letters to solve the clue.

1. You might eat this on your birthday.	c ____ k ____
2. You do this with your teeth.	b ____ t ____
3. Where you live.	h ____ m ____
4. It flies in the air.	pl ____ n ____
5. To jump into water. *Splash!*	d ____ v ____
⭐ **6.** Very big.	h ____ g ____
⭐ **7.** It is white, and you eat it.	r ____ c ____

Missing Letters

Name: _____ Date: _____

What's My Word?
Long *a*

Directions: Read each clue. Look at the incomplete word. Write the missing letters to solve the clue.

1. You can ride on this. *Choo! Choo!*	tr ____ ____ n
2. You do this with a game.	pl ____ ____
3. This food is purple or green.	gr ____ p ____ s
4. You do this with a brush.	p ____ ____ nt
5. It is a color.	gr ____ ____
⭐ 6. This is the name of a country.	Sp ____ ____ n
⭐ 7. You can color with this.	cr ____ ____ on

Missing Letters

Name: _____   Date: _____

What's My Word?
Long e

Directions: Read each clue. Look at the incomplete word. Write the missing letters to solve the clue.

1. It is the color of grass.	gr ____ ____ n
2. This place has sand and shells.	b ____ ____ ch
3. A kid under one year old.	bab ____
4. Places where people live.	cit ____ ____ s
5. You might do this when you sleep.	dr ____ ____ m
⭐ **6.** A plant that grows in the ocean.	s ____ ____ w ____ ____ d
⭐ **7.** A number.	sixt ____ ____ n

Missing Letters

Name: _____   Date: _____

What's My Word?
Long o

Directions: Read each clue. Look at the incomplete word. Write the missing letters to solve the clue.

#	Clue	Word
1.	You wear this when it's cold.	c ____ ____ t
2.	It is white, fluffy, and cold.	sn ____ ____
3.	Cars go on this.	r ____ ____ d
4.	To get bigger.	gr ____ ____
5.	You have 10 of these on your feet.	t ____ ____ s
6. ⭐	You see it in the sky after a rainstorm.	rainb ____ ____
7. ⭐	This is a food you can eat for breakfast.	____ ____ tmeal

Missing Letters

Name: _____ Date: _____

What's My Word?
Long *i*

Directions: Read each clue. Look at the incomplete word. Write the missing letters to solve the clue.

1. You can ride this.	b ___ k ___
2. You turn this on when it's dark.	l ___ ___ ___ t
3. Not day.	n ___ ___ ___ t
4. It can have clouds in it.	sk ___
5. A kid.	ch ___ ld
6. ⭐ A food you can eat.	p ___ ___
7. ⭐ A road with lots of cars.	h ___ ___ ___ way

Missing Letters

Name: _____   Date: _____

What's My Word?
Long *u*

Directions: Read each clue. Look at the incomplete word. Write the missing letters to solve the clue.

1. Pretty.	c __ t __
2. Very big.	h __ g __
3. Not a lot.	f __ __
4. You order from this at a restaurant.	men __
5. You listen to this.	m __ sic
6. ⭐ When you fight with someone, you ___.	arg __ __
7. ⭐ To save someone.	resc __ __

The Megabook of Spelling: Grades K–2 © Wiley Blevins, Scholastic Inc.

Missing Letters

Name: _____   Date: _____

What's My Word?
r-Controlled Vowels er, ir, ur

Directions: Read each clue. Look at the incomplete word. Write the missing letters to solve the clue.

1. An animal that flies.	b _____ _____ d
2. Something hot can _____ you.	b _____ _____ n
3. Not a boy.	g _____ _____ l
4. Not over, but _____.	und _____ _____
5. You wear this.	sh _____ _____ t
⭐ 6. Not brother, but _____.	sist _____ _____
⭐ 7. A slow animal.	t _____ _____ tle

Name: _____   Date: _____

What's My Word?
r-Controlled Vowel *ar*

Directions: Read each clue. Look at the incomplete word. Write the missing letters to solve the clue.

#	Clue	Word
1.	It shines in the night sky.	st __ __
2.	Horses live in this.	b __ __ n
3.	Big.	l __ __ ge
4.	A month.	M __ __ ch
5.	An animal with sharp teeth.	sh __ __ k
6. ★	The space behind a house.	backy __ __ d
7. ★	An instrument.	guit __ __

Missing Letters

Missing Letters

Name: _____ Date: _____

What's My Word?
r-Controlled Vowels or, ore, oar, oor, our

Directions: Read each clue. Look at the incomplete word. Write the missing letters to solve the clue.

1.	You use this when eating.	f ____ ____ k
2.	You open this to go in a room.	d ____ ____ ____
3.	Not less, but ____.	m ____ r ____
4.	This is an animal you can ride.	h ____ ____ se
5.	Bad weather.	st ____ ____ m
⭐ 6.	A number.	f ____ ____ ____
⭐ 7.	The sound a lion makes.	r ____ ____ ____

Missing Letters

Name: _____ Date: _____

What's My Word?
r-Controlled Vowels *air, ear, ere, are*

Directions: Read each clue. Look at the incomplete word. Write the missing letters to solve the clue.

1.	You sit in this.	ch ___ ___ ___
2.	An animal.	b ___ ___ ___
3.	A question word.	wh ___ ___ ___
4.	A fruit.	p ___ ___ ___
5.	Two of one thing.	p ___ ___ ___
⭐ 6.	Not common.	r ___ ___ ___
⭐ 7.	To fix something broken.	rep ___ ___ ___

The Megabook of Spelling: Grades K–2 © Wiley Blevins, Scholastic Inc.

Missing Letters

Name: _____ Date: _____

What's My Word?
Diphthongs *oi, oy*

Directions: Read each clue. Look at the incomplete word. Write the missing letters to solve the clue.

1.	Not a girl.	b ___ ___
2.	To heat water.	b ___ ___ l
3.	You play with this.	t ___ ___
4.	You do this with your finger.	p ___ ___ nt
5.	A loud sound.	n ___ ___ se
⭐ 6.	To have fun.	enj ___ ___
⭐ 7.	To tear something down.	destr ___ ___

Missing Letters

Name: _____ Date: _____

What's My Word?
Diphthongs *ou, ow*

Directions: Read each clue. Look at the incomplete word. Write the missing letters to solve the clue.

1.	You can live in this.	h __ __ se
2.	A small city.	t __ __ n
3.	It is white and fluffy in the sky.	cl __ __ d
4.	To yell.	sh __ __ t
5.	Not up.	d __ __ n
⭐ 6.	The hair above your eye.	eyebr __ __
⭐ 7.	To say a word.	pron __ __ nce

Missing Letters

Name: _____   Date: _____

What's My Word?
Complex Vowel /ô/ a, au, aw

Directions: Read each clue. Look at the incomplete word. Write the missing letters to solve the clue.

#	Clue	Word
1.	You can put this on noodles, like spaghetti.	s __ __ ce
2.	A nail on a bird's foot.	cl __ __
3.	To say something.	t __ lk
4.	Not big.	sm __ ll
5.	You can do this with a pencil.	dr __ __
6. ★	A kind of animal that is no longer alive.	dinos __ __ r
7. ★	A month.	__ __ gust

208   The Megabook of Spelling: Grades K–2 © Wiley Blevins, Scholastic Inc.

Name: _____   Date: _____

What's My Word?
Short *oo*

Directions: Read each clue. Look at the incomplete word. Write the missing letters to solve the clue.

1.	You read this.	b ___ ___ k
2.	Houses can be made of this.	w ___ ___ d
3.	You can do this with food.	c ___ ___ k
4.	This is at the bottom of your leg.	f ___ ___ t
5.	Not bad.	g ___ ___ d
⭐ 6.	You collect things in this.	scrapb ___ ___ k
⭐ 7.	You can eat this yummy treat.	c ___ ___ kie

Missing Letters

Name: _____ Date: _____

What's My Word?
Long oo (oo, ew, ue, u_e, oe)

Directions: Read each clue. Look at the incomplete word. Write the missing letters to solve the clue.

1.	You see this in the night sky.	m ___ ___ n
2.	You sweep with this.	br ___ ___ m
3.	Not old.	n ___ ___
4.	A color.	bl ___ ___
5.	A month.	J ___ n ___
⭐ 6.	You can fill this with air.	ball ___ ___ n
⭐ 7.	You wear this on your feet.	sh ___ ___

210 The Megabook of Spelling: Grades K–2 © Wiley Blevins, Scholastic Inc.

What's My Word?
Silent Letters

Directions: Read each clue. Look at the incomplete word. Write the missing letters to solve the clue.

1.	You do this with a pencil.	____ ____ ite
2.	You cut things with this.	____ ____ ife
3.	Not right or correct.	____ ____ ong
4.	A part of your leg.	____ ____ ee
5.	A baby sheep.	lam ____
⭐ 6.	Something with a store's name on it.	si ____ n
⭐ 7.	Past tense of *can*.	cou ____ d

Missing Letters

What's My Word?

Prefixes -un, -re and Suffixes -ful, -less

Directions: Read each clue. Look at the incomplete word. Write the missing letters to solve the clue.

1.	Not happy.	___ ___ happy
2.	To cook again.	___ ___ cook
3.	The opposite of *tie*.	___ ___ tie
4.	To have lots of hope.	hope ___ ___ ___
5.	To be without hope.	hope ___ ___ ___ ___
⭐ 6.	Very pretty.	beauti ___ ___ ___
⭐ 7.	If something won't hurt you, it is ___.	harm ___ ___ ___ ___

Activity 5: Word Ladders

Word ladders, popularized by Dr. Timothy Rasinski, are another way to practice spelling using a chain of related words. Each rung of the word ladder provides a vocabulary (meaning) clue as children go from word to word. The clues also tell how many letters to add, delete, or change. See the sample below and the customizable templates that follow. Use the word chains in Section 4 for possible word lists.

Section 6
Word-Building Center

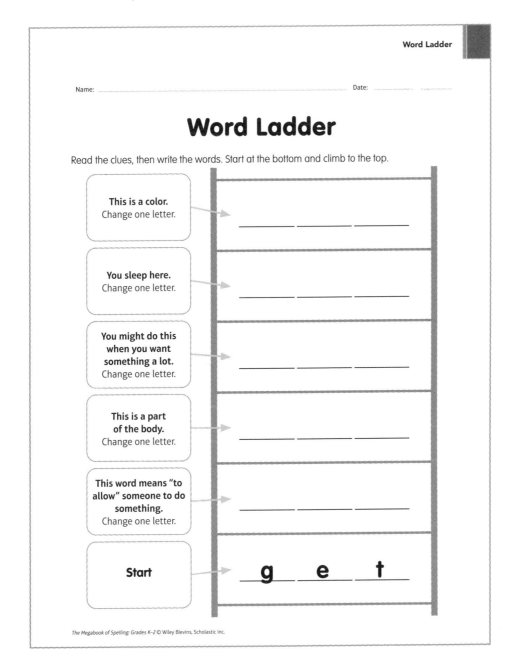

Word Ladder

Name: _____   Date: _____

Word Ladder (1)

Read the clues, then write the words. Start at the bottom and climb to the top.

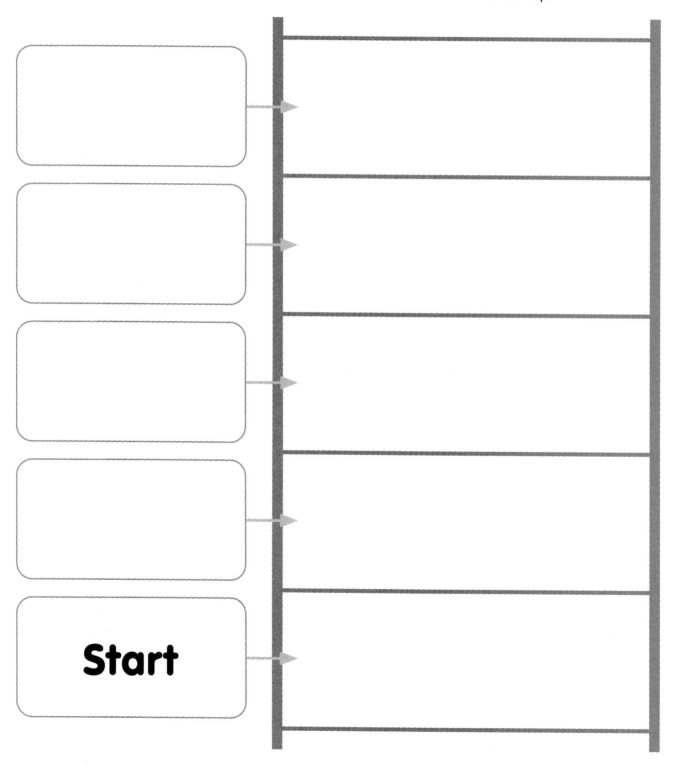

Name: _____ Date: _____

Word Ladder (2)

Read the clues, then write the words. Start at the bottom and climb to the top.

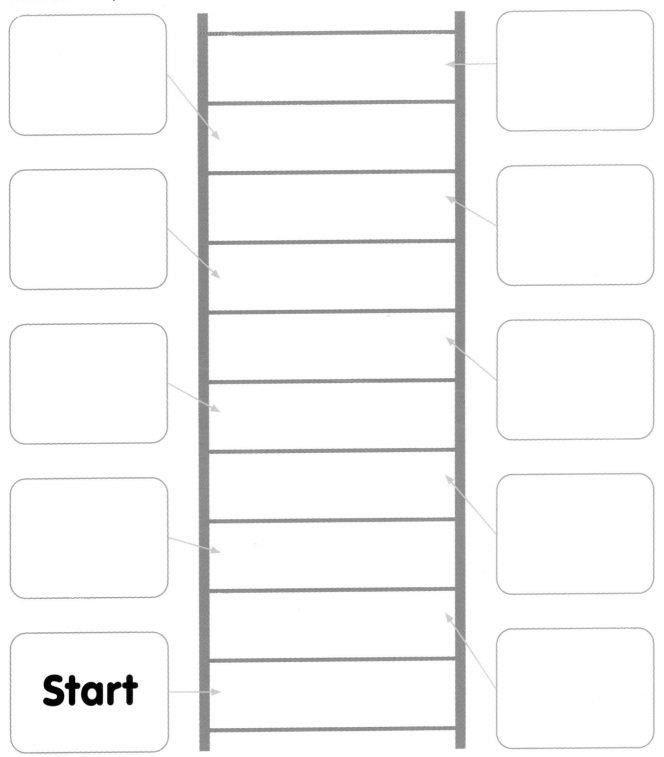

Section 6
Word-Building Center

Section 6 downloadables are available here.

Other Word-Building Activities

Activity 6: Scrambled Words
Provide a word bank on the board. Use words from your weekly decodable texts or spelling lists. Then, give children a set of scrambled words to unscramble. This requires them to attend to each letter/spelling in a word and notice spelling patterns. Some children find scrambled words challenging, so offer the first letter (or first and last) as support.

Activity 7: Crossword Puzzles
Crossword puzzles make good spelling practice because they require children to attend to each letter in a word and have an added benefit—vocabulary work. Scan the QR code at left for websites that let you make your own.

Activity 8: Word Searches
Word searches also make good spelling practice because they require children to attend to each letter or spelling pattern in a word. Children repeat this pattern over and over in their minds as they look for the word in the word search (e.g., *b-o-a-t, b-o-a-t, b-o-a-t, b-o-a-t*... Ahhh! There it is: *boat*). Scan the QR code at left for websites that let you make your own.

SECTION 7

Teach Phonics to Mastery: Scope and Sequence

Principle 2: Phonics and Handwriting Fluency

Skills Practiced

- Phonemic Awareness ☐
- Handwriting ☐
- Spelling ☐
- Decoding ☐
- Dictation ☐
- Writing ☐

For children to spell well, they must learn the most frequent spellings for each sound in English. This is accomplished through explicit phonics instruction in the first few years of school. It takes longer for children to transfer spellings into writing than reading, so they will need more and continued focus well past the initial introduction of a phonics skill. Simultaneously, children need to develop handwriting fluency—the automatic formation of letters. Activities in kindergarten in which children practice writing the letters of the alphabet as they say each letter's most common sound can accelerate and solidify this learning. Teachers typically review letter-sounds briefly at the beginnings of lessons using letter and spelling cards. Children see the letter or spelling and chorally state the sound. The reverse should also happen as a daily warm-up. The teacher should say a sound and ask children to write the letter or spelling (sometimes multiple spellings) for that sound. The teacher can reinforce proper letter formation during this activity. Some children struggle with where to start forming a letter and how to correctly form it.

If you need a scope and sequence, here are some guiding principles and a recommended sequence. While there is no right or best scope and sequence, there are sequences that are easier for children because they progress from the known to the new in simple steps instead of great conceptual leaps.

Scope and sequences are built on many criteria, such as separating confusing letters and sounds, consulting grade-level standards, and looking at the utility of spellings. However, creators of scope and sequences for instructional programs don't always take into consideration the conceptual knowledge needed by children as they progress from skill to skill. This sometimes results in big conceptual leaps from one skill to the next and a mix of key phonics concepts that can add to children's confusion about how English words work. The conceptual sequence below avoids those issues.

Concept 1: One Letter, One Sound

Consonants and Short Vowels: VC (*up*) and CVC (*man*) words

Begin with the simplest concept: one letter standing for one sound. This is generally the first concept taught in kindergarten using short-vowel sounds.

Consonant Blends (Clusters): *l*-blends, *s*-blends, *r*-blends, ending blends

Progress to consonant blends in which the big change is the inclusion of one more letter. Some scope and sequences prefer to teach consonant digraphs (e.g., *sh, ch, th, wh, ph*) before consonant blends, but jumping conceptually to two letters standing for one sound, then returning back to one letter for one sound confuses some children.

Using minimal contrasts (e.g., *cap/clap, top/stop, rip/trip, sing/sting/string, sad/sand*), going from the known to the new, more easily draws children's attention to the new learning.

Section 7

Teach Phonics to Mastery: Scope and Sequence

The selection and sequence of words in phonics activities can make a difference. They can allow you to contrast concepts and spark important conversations about how words work (e.g., *What do you hear that's different in these two words? What do you see that's different?*). Many children need extra support with ending blends so these contrasts can be very beneficial.

Concept 2: Two or More Letters, One Sound and Spelling (except /ch/ spelled *ch/tch*)

Consonant Digraphs: *sh, ch, tch, wh, ph, th, ng*

The next big conceptual leap is teaching children that two or more letters together can represent one sound. Begin with consonant digraphs because the two letters appear side by side in the word and their sound-spelling correspondences are generally consistent.

Again, contrasts (e.g., *hop/shop/chop, hat/that/chat*), going from the known to the new, more easily draw children's attention to the new learning. They can allow you to contrast concepts and spark important conversations about how words work (e.g., *What do you hear that's different in these two words? What do you see that's different?*).

You can teach both *ng* (digraph) and *nk* (blend) together and as spelling patterns (e.g., *-ing, -ink, -ung, -unk*) because these spellings are quite difficult for young learners, especially when segmenting words. Although you might have learned a lot about linguistics, it isn't necessary to share everything with very young students as it can overcomplicate their learning.

Final e: *a_e, i_e, o_e, e_e, u_e*

Final *e* (or silent *e*) spellings also fall into this conceptual category. However, they are more complex because the two letters working together aren't beside each other in the word. That's a huge conceptual leap for young learners.

Again, contrasts (e.g., *hat/hate, rid/ride, hop/hope*), going from the known to the new, more easily draw children's attention to the new learning. Ask these questions to spark conversation about how English words work and why this spelling is so important to deeply understand: *What do you hear that's different in these two words? What do you see that's different?*

Concept 3: Two or More Letters, One Sound . . . but Multiple Spellings

Vowel Digraphs: Long *a, e, i, o, u*

The next big conceptual leap is teaching children that two or more letters together can represent one sound, but there are now multiple spellings for that sound. Unlike with the relative consistency of consonant-digraph spellings, children need to learn and more carefully examine where in words these long-vowel spellings appear. For example, the long-*a* spelling *ai* never appears at the end of a word, but the *ay* spelling does. This deeper and more complex knowledge of sound-spellings is necessary to help children develop strong spelling skills.

Again, contrasts (e.g., *ran/rain*), going from the known to the new, more easily draw children's attention to the new learning. Many state standards require children to distinguish long-vowel and short-vowel sounds. This knowledge is also important when children begin learning about syllable types (e.g., closed syllables that have a short-vowel sound and open syllables that have a long-vowel sound). Ask these questions to spark conversation about how English words work and why this spelling is so important to deeply understand: *What do you hear that's different in these two words? What do you see that's different?*

At this conceptual level, it will be important to expand children's knowledge of which letters can be used to represent vowel sounds in writing. For example, teach children the long-*e* spellings *e, ee, ea, y, ey* and the long-*o* spellings *o, oa, ow*. Children must be explicitly taught that consonants like *y* and *w* can act as vowels in vowel spellings like *ey* and *ow*.

Diphthongs: *oi/oy, ou/ow*

Long-vowel sounds are generally easier to pronounce and stable in terms of their articulation. That is, we can easily show and describe the position of the mouth when making the sound. Diphthongs pose a new challenge. These glide sounds create movement in the mouth when they are formed. Try it. Say the long-*e* sound /ē/ and hold it. You look like you are smiling. Now look in the mirror and say the /ou/ sound. Notice how your mouth moves when making the sound. This can make spelling words with these sounds more difficult for early writers. (**Note:** Long *i* is technically also a glide sound. Feel it as you make the sound. Notice how your mouth moves.)

r-Controlled Vowels: *ar, or/oar/ore, er, ir, ur*

Another conceptual complexity is learning how letters, such as *r* after a vowel, can affect the vowel sound. While there are multiple letters that do this, *r*-controlled vowel spellings are most commonly taught because of their high utility in reading and writing words. Instead of the vowel sound being long or short, it's a modified sound that children need to learn.

Again, contrasts (e.g., *cat/car*), going from the known to the new, more easily draw children's attention to the new learning. You can use these contrasts to compare, for example, the short-vowel sound in *cat* with the *r*-controlled vowel sound in *car*.

Some programs refer to *r*-controlled vowel spellings as one sound. I do not. These spellings contain a vowel and a consonant—two sounds (the affected vowel sound and the /r/ sound for *r*). However, these spellings are extremely difficult to orally separate, and some programs refer to them as "glued sounds" as a result. So, when doing oral-segmentation exercises (like the ones on pages 48–51), for example, have children keep the spelling in the same box. Again, there is no reason to make things overly complex for our early learners.

Other Complex Vowels: *oo, aw, al(k), al(t), al(l)*

Finally, address other complex vowel sounds and their multiple spellings. Some of these, such as long *oo*, have so many spellings that we must be cautious about how many to introduce at one time. In fact, most of the skills in Concept 3 are taught in Grade 1, with a higher concentration in the second half of the grade. The large number of spellings can be too much too fast for some children. These skills should be reviewed in the beginning of Grade 2 for most children, and books and activities focusing on them are ideal for summer-school reading and writing. You can teach the less-common spellings incidentally as they appear in books read.

Section 7

Teach Phonics to Mastery: Scope and Sequence

Concept 4: Multisyllabic Words

After teaching Concepts 1, 2, and 3 using one-syllable words, progress to transitioning children to reading multisyllabic words. This is where basic phonics instruction becomes word study instruction. *Word study* refers to the process of learning everything about words, including their spelling, meaning, pronunciation, historical origin, and relationship with other words. It requires use of phonics, context clues, and structural analysis of word parts to determine both meaning and pronunciation. It extends beyond spelling. Children who are on-grade level know far too little about the major structures of words, including syllable and morpheme patterns. This instruction, however, improves children's ability to interpret (sound out), remember the meanings of, and spell new multisyllabic words. These are some of the key skills to address:

- Syllable types (e.g., open, closed, consonant + *le*)
- Prefixes
- Suffixes
- Greek and Latin roots (morphology)

A Note About Morphology

Once we get to multisyllabic words, morphology begins to play a far more important role in understanding and remembering how a word is spelled because English is a morphophonemic language. The *morpheme* is the smallest unit of meaning in a word, and its spelling across related words is generally stable even when the pronunciation varies. Pointing out the spelling consistency across morphemes is vital to children advancing in spelling development. Below are a few examples to illustrate this.

- **sign/signal/signature:** explain why the *g* in *sign* is necessary
- **soft/soften, limb/limber:** explain additional silent letter inclusion in words
- **different/difference, fragrant/fragrance:** comparing related words helps children determine whether to use *-ent* or *-ence* when spelling
- **act/action, tense/tension, equate/equation:** comparing related words helps children determine whether to use *-tion* or *-sion* when spelling even when pronunciation changes
- **do/doing/does, be/being/been, play/plays/stay/stays/say/says:** comparing related words helps children determine spelling even when pronunciation changes

Note: Spelling also helps clarify and distinguish homophones as in the following examples:

- *days* (plural of *day*) versus *daze*
- *by* (uses *y*, like in *why/try/sky*, because English words don't end in *i*), *bye* (related to *good-bye* from the Old English saying "God be with *ye*"), and *buy* (*u* is the homophone marker and connects it to the past tense *bought*)

Scope and Sequence Conceptual Summary

Create and use a phonics scope and sequence that builds from the known to the new in small conceptual steps rather than large or sporadic conceptual leaps common to many scope and sequences in current phonics programs.

1. Short-Vowel CVC Words • Short *a* • Short *i* • Short *o* • Short *u* • Short *e*	1 Letter, 1 Sound
2. Short-Vowel Words with Consonant Blends • *l*-blends • *s*-blends • *r*-blends • 3-letter blends • ending blends	1 Letter, 1 Sound
3. Short-Vowel Words with Consonant Digraphs • *sh* • *ch/tch* • *th* (both sounds) • *wh* • *ng* (add blend *nk*) • *ph*	2+ Letters, 1 Sound, 1 Spelling
4. Final e • *a_e* • *i_e* • *o_e* • *u_e* and *e_e* (not many one-syllable words)	2+ Letters, 1 Sound, 1 Spelling
5. Long Vowels (most common spellings) • Long *a* (*a, ai, ay*) • Long *e* (*e, ee, ea, ie, ey, y*) • Long *o* (*o, oa, ow, oe*) • Long *i* (*i, igh, y*) • Long *u* (*u_e, ew, ue*) (not many simple words and these spellings have multiple sounds)	2+ Letters, 1 Sound, Multiple Spellings
6. Complex Vowels • *r*-controlled vowels (*ar, or, er, ir, ur*) • Diphthongs (*ou, ow; oi, oy*) • Long *oo* (*o, oo, u_e, ue, ew*) and short *oo* (*oo, u*) • Complex vowel /ô/ (*a, a(ll), a(lk), a(lt), au, aw*)	2+ Letters, 1 Sound, Multiple Spellings
7. Multisyllabic Words • Prefixes • Suffixes • Syllable types	2+ Syllables

Section 7

Teach Phonics to Mastery: Scope and Sequence

Section 7

Teach Phonics to Mastery: Scope and Sequence

Set for Variability: FLEX IT!

Once children learn multiple spellings for one sound, it is important to model how to use this knowledge flexibly to read and write words. For example, if children read the word *thread* with the long-*e* sound because that is the most common sound for that spelling that they have learned, model how to use the short-*e* sound to correctly pronounce the word. Say: *What other sound have we learned for the* ea *spelling, like in the word* head?

This flexible modeling will also carry over to spelling. For example, if children spell the word *his* as *h-i-z*, say: *What other letter have we learned for the /z/ sound at the end of a word, like in the word* is?

In addition, repeatedly reinforcing where certain spellings appear in words can help children make better-informed choices when spelling. For example, if children spell the word *train* as *t-r-a-y-n*, say: *Remember, the* ay *spelling for the long-*a *sound /ā/ only appears at the end of a word or syllable; we can use the* ai *spelling when the long-*a *sound /ā/ is in the middle of a word.*

Sample Spelling Teaching Points

Skill Category	Sample Teaching Points
Short Vowels	• **ea** for **short e** (*head, dead, bread*), **long e** (*read, team*), and **long a** (*great, break*)—sometimes readers must try a different sound for **ea** to arrive at the correct word. It's important to model this.
Consonant Blends	• Clearly articulate blends in words, especially ending blends, and have children repeat. Use sound boxes or tapping to mark and count each sound before spelling. • **ck** used at the end of a word when it follows a single short vowel. Note: **k** at the beginning when followed by *e* (*kept/key*) or *i* (*king*); **c** at the beginning when followed by *a* (*cat*), *o* (*cot, coat*), *u* (*cut*)
Consonant Digraphs and Trigraphs	• **tch** at the end of a word when it follows a single short vowel (*witch, patch*); **ch** at the end of a word when it follows a consonant or vowel team (*bench, reach, couch*) • **th** has two sounds: voiced (*them*) and unvoiced (*thin*) • It's easier to teach **ng** (and the blend **nk**) in spelling patterns such as *-ing, -ink, -ang, -ank, -ung, -unk*. • **dge** used only after a single short vowel (*judge*)
Final *e*	• Point out exception words, such as those ending in **ve** (*have, give, live, love*—no English words end in *v*) and *come/some* (perhaps related to the word's history and earlier pronunciation or connect it to a related word, as in *come/came, some/same*).

Long Vowels	• ***ai*** in the middle of a word (*rain*) and ***ay*** at the end of a word or syllable (*play*—English words don't end in *i*; notable exceptions are *taxi*, which is a clipped word from *taxicab*, and *ski*, which is a foreign word)
	• ***a*** and ***e*** in an open syllable within a word (*ta/ble, be/cause*). Note that ***a*** at the beginning of many words is in an unaccented syllable and has the schwa sound (*ago, about, around*).
	• ***oa*** in the middle of a word (*boat*) and ***ow*** at the end of a word or syllable (*snow*). Note that ***ow*** can stand for **long o** or /**ou**/ (*now, down*).
	• ***igh*** is the full **long-i** spelling; ***ie*** (*pie, tie*) is used because English words don't end in *i*; ***y*** can stand for **long i** in one-syllable words (*my, try, cry*) or **long e** in longer words (*funny, silly*). The long-*i* sound is categorized as a diphthong by linguists because of the gliding movement in the mouth when making the sound.
Diphthongs	• ***ou*** in the middle of a word (*round*—no English words end in *u* unless a clipped word or foreign word, like *flu/influenza*, and ***ow*** at the end of a word or syllable or when followed by *n* (*now, down*). Note that ***ow*** can stand for **long o** (*snow*) or /**ou**/.
	• ***ouse*** words add an *e* so that the word does not look like a plural (*hous* vs. *house*)
	• ***oi*** in the middle of a word (*soil*) and ***oy*** at the end of a word or syllable (no English words end in *i*)
r-Controlled Vowels	• There is no rule to remember when to use ***er/ir/ur***—children need lots of exposure to these words in print and a focus on the common spelling patterns (*-urn, -irl*). Note that we generally use ***er*** at the end of a multisyllabic word (*never, winter, farmer*). When dictating words, connect the spelling to known words (for example, this word has the same /ûr/ spelling as in *bird*).
	• ***or*** is usually in the middle of a word (*former, born*) and ***ore*** at the end (*store, more, score*); ***oar*** isn't as commonly used.
Other Complex Vowels	• ***au*** in the middle of a word (*sauce*—no English words end in *u*) and ***aw*** at the end of a word or syllable (*saw*). When ***wa*** starts a word the sound for *a* is /ô/.
	• Teach the long-*oo* spellings in families: ***oom/oon/ood, ew*** (*chew, knew, blew*), ***ue*** (*blue/glue/true*). Note position and that English words don't end in *i* or *u* and discuss homophone markers (*blue/blew*).
Prefixes	• Point out that prefixes are a separate syllable and focus on using the meaning of the prefix to determine the whole word's meaning.
Suffixes	• Focus on spelling changes when adding suffixes (drop *e*, change *y* to *i*, double final consonant) and identifying the base word when a suffix is removed (especially when a letter is dropped or changes—*like/liking, take/taking*—which can confuse children when reading and spelling).

Principle 3: Print Exposure Through Decodable Texts

Skills Practiced

Phonemic Awareness

Handwriting

Spelling

Decoding

Dictation

Writing

Section 8 downloadables are available here.

SECTION 8

Write About Decodable Texts

Decodable texts, in which a high percentage of the words contain taught phonics patterns, are used in the early grades to build fluency reading words with these patterns. These repeated readings have an additional benefit: Seeing these patterns in many words over and over builds statistical awareness of how these spelling patterns are used in words and can accelerate children's awareness of and use of these patterns when writing (spelling).

Writing about a decodable text offers a unique opportunity to combine comprehension and encoding practice for children. As children write, they show their developing understanding of the story while engaging in a structured exercise that requires them to use decodable words with the new target phonics skill. This encourages learners to reread the text as they write, which benefits both their reading and their spelling. The words and sentences in the decodable text give children a "running start" on their writing, making the task of composing ideas less daunting for them.

- Have children write about every decodable text they read.
- Don't approach these writings as one-off assignments. Revisit the writings on subsequent days, and have children revise them based on aspects of writing you are teaching in your writing lessons at other times during your literacy block, such as correcting punctuation or capitalization errors, combining sentences, or adding more vivid verbs.
- Many children need more structure and support with writing about texts than is provided in most curriculum. These supports include word banks, sentence frames, paragraph frames (fiction retelling, nonfiction summary), and aid in writing constructed responses (e.g., writing the gist sentence on one day, then rereading the story next day and adding two details).

Materials Needed	The following pages provide guided practice in using decodable texts as springboards to writing. • Pages 225–228 feature sample decodable texts and model writing extensions. • Pages 229–242 provide writing-response templates for decodable texts. • Page 243 offers a revision checklist for children to check their own writing.
Length of Activity	10–15 minutes
Location	school or home

Let's Grow Them

"What's that?" said Jess.

"Ten seeds," said Ben. "Let's grow them."

Ben and Jess dig and dig and dig and dig.

The seeds are in!

Ben gets a can.

Jess gets a hose.

The seeds get wet.

Ben and Jess sit and sit.

They sit and sit.

"Will the seeds grow?" said Jess.

"They will grow," said Ben.

"Will they get big?" said Jess.

"They will get big," said Ben.

"Will they get red?" said Jess.

"Yes," said Ben. "You will see."

Time passes . . .

"See the big, red tomatoes," said Ben.

"Yes!" said Jess. "Yum!"

Writing Response

Name: _____ Date: _____

Retell It

_____

Retell what Jess and Ben do to grow tomatoes.

First, _____

_____

Next, _____

_____

Then, _____

_____

At last, _____

_____

All Around the Farm

Steve is a farmer. Steve grows corn on a farm in Maine. He likes life on the farm.

Steve rises before the sun comes up and goes to the fields. There is a lot to do every day on a farm.

He bends down to feel the rich, brown ground. The sun is up now, and it feels hot on his back. It's a good day to plant some corn!

Steve uses a machine to help him. It drops seeds into the ground. A wheel packs the seeds down deep.

The corn seeds need a lot of sun and water. Soon sprouts will come out. Then the corn will grow until it is very tall.

Look how tall it is now! Steve will teach his son about growing corn. One day his son will help him.

Now Steve wants to see if the corn is ripe. He rips off an ear of corn to take a look at it.

He peels back the thick green husk. The corn inside is round and yellow. It is ready to pick.

Steve uses a big machine to pick the corn. It goes up and down the tall fields, picking corn along the way.

Big and little ears of corn fill a truck. The truck takes them to a shed where the corn is packed in boxes.

Then Steve puts each box on a big truck. This truck will take the corn to places near and far.

When the sun goes down, it's time for a yummy farm meal. There is meat, beets, beans, and lots of corn!

How does the corn get from the farm to your house?

1. Plant the corn.
2. Grow the corn.
3. Pick the corn.
4. Pack the corn.
5. Go to the store and get the corn.
6. Eat the corn. Yum!

Writing Response

Name: _____ Date: _____

The Big Idea

Tell what Steve does on the farm.

_____

_____

_____

_____

Writing Response

Name: _____ Date: _____

Just the Gist: Fiction (1)

Tell what the story is mostly about. Fill in each section.

_____   _____
   (Who?)   (Did What?)

Writing Response

Name: _____ Date: _____

Just the Gist: Fiction (2)

Tell what the story is mostly about. Fill in each section.

_____   _____
(Who?)   (Did What?)

_____
(Where?)

Writing Response

Name: _____ Date: _____

Just the Gist: Fiction (3)

Tell what the story is mostly about. Fill in each section.

_____ _____
(Who?)   (Did What?)

_____
(When?)

Writing Response

Name: _____ Date: _____

Just the Gist: Fiction (4)

Tell what the story is mostly about. Fill in each section.

_____ _____
(Who?) (Did What?)

_____
(Where?)

_____
(When?)

Writing Response

Name: _____ Date: _____

Just the Gist: Fiction (5)

```
┌─────────────────────────────────────────┐
│                                         │
│                                         │
│                                         │
│                                         │
│                                         │
│                                         │
│                                         │
└─────────────────────────────────────────┘
```

Tell what the story is mostly about. Fill in each section.

_____   _____
     (Who?)   (Did What?)

_____
                    (Where?)

_____
                     (Why?)

Writing Response

Name: _____ Date: _____

Just the Gist: Fiction (6)

[box   ]

Tell what the story is mostly about. Fill in each section.

_____   _____
(Who?)   (Did What?)

_____
(Where?)

_____
(When?)

_____
(Why?)

Writing Response

Name: _____ Date: _____

Just the Gist: Nonfiction (I)

```
┌─────────────────────────────────────────────┐
│                                             │
│                                             │
│                                             │
│                                             │
│                                             │
│                                             │
│                                             │
│                                             │
└─────────────────────────────────────────────┘
```

Tell what the text is mostly about.

The main topic of _____ is _____.

One detail is _____

_____.

Another detail is _____

_____.

The Megabook of Spelling: Grades K–2 © Wiley Blevins, Scholastic Inc.   235

Writing Response

Name: _____ Date: _____

Just the Gist: Nonfiction (2)

Tell what the text is mostly about.

The text is about _____.

One thing I learned is _____

_____.

Another thing I learned is _____

_____.

Writing Response

Name: _____   Date: _____

Retell It

In the beginning of the story, _____

_____.

In the middle, _____

_____

_____.

At the end, _____

_____.

Writing Response

Name: _____ Date: _____

What I Learned

3 things I learned about _____

1. _____

_____

2. _____

_____

3. _____

_____

Writing Response

Name: _____ Date: _____

Sequence

First, _____

_____

Next, _____

_____

Then, _____

_____

At last, _____

_____

Writing Response

Name: _____   Date: _____

Cause and Effect

_____

_____ happened

because _____.

Therefore, _____

_____.

This explains why _____

_____.

Writing Response

Name: _____ Date: _____

Problem and Solution

```
┌─────────────────────────────────────────┐
│                                         │
│                                         │
│                                         │
│                                         │
│                                         │
│                                         │
└─────────────────────────────────────────┘
```

The problem was that _____

_____.

This problem happened because _____

_____.

The problem was finally solved when _____

_____.

Writing Response

Name: _____ Date: _____

Compare and Contrast

[   ]

Both _____ and _____

are similar in many ways. They are similar because _____

_____.

They are also similar because _____

_____.

In some ways, though, _____ and _____ are different.

They are different because _____ is _____

_____.

So, _____ and _____ have both similarities and differences.

Revision Checklist

Name: _____ Date: _____

PUSH Your Writing to the Next Level

Punctuation	. ? !	☐
Usage	two men runs̷	☐
Spelling	~~wuz~~ was	☐
Handwriting		☐

The Megabook of Spelling: Grades K–2 © Wiley Blevins, Scholastic Inc.

Principle 3: Print Exposure Through Decodable Texts

Skills Practiced

Phonemic Awareness ☐

Handwriting ☐

Spelling ☑

Decoding ☑

Dictation ☐

Writing ☑

Section 9 downloadables are available here.

SECTION 9

Syntax: Building Complex Sentences

Use decodable texts (in which a high percentage of the words contain taught phonics patterns) in the early grades to build fluency reading words with these patterns. These repeated readings have an additional benefit: Seeing these patterns in many words over and over builds statistical awareness of how these spelling patterns are used in words and can accelerate children's awareness of and use of these patterns when writing.

Writing Complex Sentences

In addition to the retelling (fiction) and summary (nonfiction text structures) writing frames in Section 8, children can use the "gist frames" in this section to check on their comprehension when time is limited. These frames help children learn how to write more complex sentences earlier in their writing development by examining sentence syntax. These frames focus on the key parts of sentences that answer the questions: Who? Did/Does what? When? Where? Why? How?

Select a frame that can be used to capture the gist of a story children just read. Slowly increase the complexity of the gist frames over time. You can also use these frames to help children combine sentences and move around sentence parts to change sentences from "book language" to "oral language" (and vice versa) when sentences are complex for children to understand.

Materials Needed	The following pages provide guided practice in using knowledge of sentence syntax to write more complex sentences that check children's comprehension of decodable text readings and offer them authentic opportunities to apply spelling skills. • Pages 245–253 offer sentence- and paragraph-building templates to create constructed responses to check understanding of decodable text readings.
Length of Activity	5–10 minutes
Location	school or home

Gist Frames

Name: _____   Date: _____

Who? Did What?

Draw a picture of the story.

_____
- -
(Who?)
_____
- -
(Did What?)

Gist Frames

Name: _____ Date: _____

Who? Did What? Where?

Draw a picture of the story.

```
┌─────────────────────────────────────┐
│                                     │
│                                     │
│                                     │
│                                     │
│                                     │
└─────────────────────────────────────┘
```

_____

(Who?)

_____

(Did What?)

_____

(Where?)

Name: _____ Date: _____

Gist Frames

Who? Did What? Where? When?

Draw a picture of the story.

_____

(Who?)   (Did What?)

_____

(Where?)

_____

(When?)

Gist Frames

Name: _____ Date: _____

Who? Did What? Where? When? Why?

Draw a picture of the story.

(Who?)

(Did What?)

(Where?)   (When?)

(Why?)

Gist Frames

Name: _____   Date: _____

Who? Did What? Where? How?

Draw a picture of the story.

```
┌─────────────────────────────────────┐
│                                     │
│                                     │
│                                     │
│                                     │
└─────────────────────────────────────┘
```

_____

(Who?)   (Did What?)

_____

(Where?)

_____

(How?)

The Megabook of Spelling: Grades K–2 © Wiley Blevins, Scholastic Inc.

Gist Frames

Name: _____   Date: _____

Flip It!

Draw a picture of the story.

```
┌─────────────────────────────────────┐
│                                     │
│                                     │
│                                     │
│                                     │
└─────────────────────────────────────┘
```

_____

(Who?)   (Did What?)

_____

(Where?)

FLIP IT!

_____

(Where?)   (Who?)

_____

(Did What?)

Gist Frames

Name: _____ Date: _____

Combine It! (I)

Draw a picture of the story.

[   ]

_____   _____
(Who?)   (Who?)

_____
(Did What?)

COMBINE IT!

_____
(Who **and** Who?)

_____
(Did What?)

Gist Frames

Name: _____   Date: _____

Combine It! (2)

Draw a picture of the story.

```
┌─────────────────────────────────────────┐
│                                         │
│                                         │
│                                         │
│                                         │
└─────────────────────────────────────────┘
```

_____

(Who?)   (Did What?)

_____

(Did What?)

COMBINE IT!

_____

(Who? Did What?)

_____

(and Did What?)

Gist Frames

Name: _____ Date: _____

Change It!

Draw a picture of the story.

[drawing box]

_____
_ _ _ _ _ _ _ _ _ _ _ _ _ _ _ _
(Statement.) _____
_____
_ _ _ _ _ _ _ _ _ _ _ _ _ _ _ _

CHANGE IT! _____
_____
_ _ _ _ _ _ _ _ _ _ _ _ _ _ _ _
(Question?) _____
_____
_ _ _ _ _ _ _ _ _ _ _ _ _ _ _ _

The Megabook of Spelling: Grades K–2 © Wiley Blevins, Scholastic Inc.

Principle 6: Assessment and Differentiated Supports

Skills Practiced

Phonemic Awareness ☐

Handwriting ☐

Spelling

Decoding

Dictation ☐

Writing

Section 10 downloadables are available here.

SECTION 10

Student Writing Evaluation Tools for Writer's Notebook

Children in any given classroom represent a range of mastery in terms of spelling. Therefore, it is necessary to assess spelling in a cumulative manner, monitor spelling whole class and individually, and provide differentiated supports. This makes teaching spelling more challenging and complex for teachers. Simple assessment structures and tools (e.g., mastery checklists, cumulative dictation sentences—all provided in this book) and differentiated activities (e.g., word chains and pyramids, from simple to complex) go a long way to better meet all children's spelling needs.

How to Use the Spelling Checklists

- At the beginning of the year, direct children to tape or paste the grade-appropriate spelling checklist (pages 256–258) into the front or back of their writer's notebook.

- When you introduce a new phonics skill, have children circle that skill on the checklist. Tell them that this means you will hold them accountable now for correctly using that skill in their writing.

- Periodically (e.g., once a month), evaluate children's most recent writings through a phonics lens. Look at the skills circled. Scan children's writing for consistent and accurate use of that skill in their spelling. If you see that progress, add a checkmark to the spelling checklist under Mastery and record a few sample words from their writings to celebrate their success when you conference with them.

- Use the results of your spelling checklist observations to provide additional whole-class lessons for phonics skills many children have yet to transfer to their writing. For skills that only a few children are struggling with, use the spelling checklist data to form skills-based small groups for additional instruction and practice through guided dictation, word building, and other high-impact encoding activities.

Materials Needed	The following pages provide teacher support in monitoring and differentiating children's spelling growth. • Pages 256–258 provide writer's notebook spelling checklists for Grades K, 1, and 2. These checklists reflect the most common skills taught at each grade level based on state standards and widely used curricular materials. Modify these checklists based on the phonics scope and sequence for your grade or reading program. • Page 259 provides a reproducible spelling goals sheet for children to set their own goals for themselves. • Page 260 presents a spelling certificate to celebrate children's achievements.
Length of Activity	5 minutes
Location	school or home

Section 10

Student Writing Evaluation Tools for Writer's Notebook

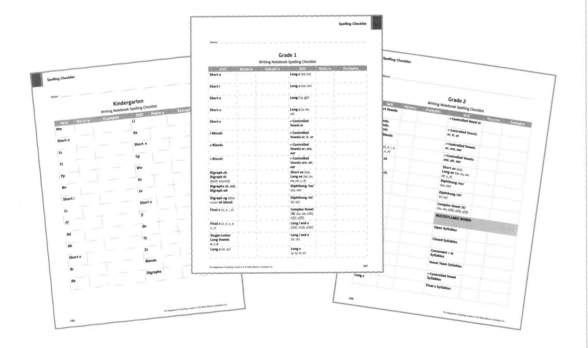

Spelling Checklist

Name: _____

Kindergarten
Writing Notebook Spelling Checklist

Skill	Mastery	Examples	Skill	Mastery	Examples
Mm			Ll		
Short *a*			Kk		
Ss			Short *e*		
Tt			Gg		
Pp			Ww		
Nn			Xx		
Short *i*			Vv		
Cc			Short *u*		
Ff			Jj		
Dd			Qu		
Hh			Yy		
Short *o*			Zz		
Rr			Blends		
Bb			Digraphs		

Spelling Checklist

Grade 1
Writing Notebook Spelling Checklist

Skill	Mastery	Examples	Skill	Mastery	Examples
Short *a*			Long *e* (*ee, ea*)		
Short *i*			Long *o* (*oa, ow*)		
Short *o*			Long *i* (*y, igh*)		
Short *u*			Long *u* (*u, ew, ue*)		
Short *e*			*r*-Controlled Vowel *ar*		
l-Blends			*r*-Controlled Vowels *er, ir, ur*		
s-Blends			*r*-Controlled Vowels *or, ore, oar*		
r-Blends			*r*-Controlled Vowels *are, air, ear*		
Digraph *sh*, Digraph *th* (both sounds)			Short *oo* (*oo*), Long *oo* (*oo, ou, ew, ue, u_e*)		
Digraphs *ch, tch*; Digraph *wh*			Diphthong /ou/ (*ou, ow*)		
Digraph *ng* (also cover *nk* blend)			Diphthong /oi/ (*oi, oy*)		
Final *e* (*a_e, i_e*)			Complex Vowel /ô/ (*au, aw, a[lk], a[lt], a[ll]*)		
Final *e* (*o_e, u_e, e_e*)			Long *i* and *o* [*i(ld), i(nd), o(ld)*]		
Single-Letter Long Vowels *e, i, o*			Long *i* and *o* (*ie, oe*)		
Long *a* (*ai, ay*)			Long *e* (*y, ey, ie, ei*)		

The Megabook of Spelling: Grades K–2 © Wiley Blevins, Scholastic Inc.

Spelling Checklist

Name: _____

Grade 2
Writing Notebook Spelling Checklist

Skill	Mastery	Examples	Skill	Mastery	Examples
Short Vowels			**r-Controlled Vowel** *ar*		
l-Blends, *r*-Blends, *s*-Blends			**r-Controlled Vowels** *er, ir, ur*		
Final Blends			**r-Controlled Vowels** *or, ore, oar*		
Final e (*a_e, i_e, o_e, e_e, u_e*)			**r-Controlled Vowels** *are, air, ear*		
Digraph *sh*			**Short oo** (*oo*), **Long oo** (*oo, ou, ew, ue, u_e*)		
Digraphs *ch, tch*			**Diphthong /ou/** (*ou, ow*)		
Digraph *th*			**Diphthong /oi/** (*oi, oy*)		
Digraph *wh*			**Complex Vowel /ô/** (*au, aw, a[lk], a[lt], a[ll]*)		
Digraph *ph*			**MULTISYLLABIC WORDS**		
Digraph *ng*/ **Blend** *nk*			**Open Syllables**		
Long *a*			**Closed Syllables**		
Long *e*			**Consonant +** *le* **Syllables**		
Long *i*			**Vowel Team Syllables**		
Long *o*			**r-Controlled Vowel Syllables**		
Long *u*			**Final e Syllables**		

Name: _____ Date: _____

My Spelling Goals

Phonics Words to Practice
(Circle target spelling patterns.)

High-Frequency Words to Practice
(Put a heart above parts to remember.)

How I Will Meet My Spelling Goals:

- [ ] I will write the word three to five times as I say the letter names out loud.

- [ ] I will look for the word and other words with the same spelling pattern when I read.

- [ ] I will collect words with the same spelling pattern and write them together in my writer's notebook. I know that paying attention to patterns across words will help me.

- [ ] I will mark parts of the word that are harder for me and focus on remembering those parts when I write. I will make up a tip to help me (such as "no words end in *v*, so I add an *e*").

I CAN SPELL!

_____ can spell phonics words with
(Student Name)

_____
(Phonics Skills)

and the high-frequency words

_____
(List of Words)

with increasing consistency and accuracy.

We love to celebrate our spelling success in _____'s classroom!
(Teacher Name)

SECTION 11

Irregular High-Frequency Words

Children should engage in encoding (spelling/writing) activities every day and in every phonics lesson. Give extra attention to the irregular high-frequency words (e.g., *said, was, they*) that many children struggle spelling because of their irregular, untaught, or less-common spelling patterns.

*Note: High-frequency words that become decodable at each point in the phonics scope and sequence should be added to dictation activities, word building, word sorts, and other places in the lessons to ensure coverage of these words as well. Since these words are decodable, the Read-Spell-Write-Extend routine (page 262) won't be necessary. Rather, model for children how to sound out these words. Also, many of the more difficult high-frequency words should be repeated throughout the grade in which they were introduced and across grades to ensure more instructional focus and intentional practice.

Materials Needed	The following pages provide guided practice in spelling irregular high-frequency words. • Pages 263–284 offer templates for spelling the 105 most commonly misspelled high-frequency words (High-Frequency Word Hurdles).
Length of Activity	5–10 minutes
Location	school or home

Principle 4: Daily Spelling and Writing Activities

Skills Practiced

Phonemic Awareness

Handwriting

Spelling

Decoding

Dictation

Writing

Section 11 downloadables are available here.

Section 11

Irregular High-Frequency Words

High-Frequency Word Routine

Use the following routine to teach high-frequency words.

Routine Steps	Sample Teacher Talk
Step 1: Read Write the word in a context sentence and underline the word. Read aloud the sentence, then point to the target underlined word and read it aloud. Have children chorally say the word. Then, to accelerate orthographic mapping, guide children to say or tap the sounds they hear in the word.	[Write and read the sentence.] "I see a cat," said Pam. [Point to the word *said*.] This is the word *said*. What is the word? (*said*) What sounds do you hear in the word *said*? Let's say them together: /s/ /e/ /d/.
Step 2: Spell Spell the word aloud and have children repeat. If children are just learning their letters, do an echo spell. Briefly point out any known spellings and then highlight the irregular, untaught, or unknown spellings that need to be remembered "by heart." Underline, write in a different color, or draw a heart above these letters.	The word *said* is spelled s-a-i-d. Spell it with me: s-a-i-d. What is the first sound in the word *said*? What letter do we write for the /s/ sound? (s) What is the last sound in the word *said*? (/d/) What letter do we write for the /d/ sound? (d) Notice that the middle /e/ sound in *said* is spelled ai. That's not how we usually spell the /e/ sound; we usually spell it with the letter e. So, that's the part of the word we will need to remember. I'm going to draw a heart above these letters to help you remember them by heart.
Step 3: Write Ask children to write the word multiple times as they spell it aloud. They can do this in the air, on dry-erase boards, or on paper. It is best to have children physically write the word with a pencil.	Watch as I write the word. I will say each letter as I write it. [Model this.] Now, it's your turn. Write the word two or three times. Say each letter as you write it.
Step 4: Extend Connect the word to other words children have learned. For example, if you have a word wall organized by spelling patterns (e.g., *could/should/would, come/some*), work with children to place the word in the correct spot on the wall. Then ask children to generate oral sentences using the word. Have them work with a partner and provide sentence frames as support, if needed. Then have children write their oral sentences. Build on these sentences as appropriate. You can do these extension activities on the days following the initial instruction when you have additional time to extend in this way.	Turn to a partner and finish this sentence: "I said _____." [Provide time for partners to share.] Now, write on your paper (or whiteboard) the sentence you just said. [Wait for children to finish.]

Name: _____ Date: _____

High-Frequency Words

Read It	Mark It	Write It
1.		
2.		
3.		
4.		
5.		

Tip: Mark the irregular, unknown, or challenging spelling to help you remember it. Circle it or draw a heart above the letter or letters.

High-Frequency Words

Name: _____ Date: _____

High-Frequency Hurdles #1

Read It	Mark It	Write It
1. could	could	
2. would	would	
3. should	should	
4. couldn't	couldn't	
5. shouldn't	shouldn't	

Tip: Teach *could*, *should*, and *would* together. Emphasize the *-ould* spelling pattern and highlight the silent *l*, which many children leave out of their spellings.

Extension: Write and have children copy and complete sentence starters such as:
I wish I could ___. At school I should ___.

Name: _____ Date: _____

High-Frequency Hurdles #2

Read It	Mark It	Write It
1. come	come	
2. some	some	
3. done	done	
4. one	one	
5. once	once	

Tip: Connect *one* to *done* and *once*. Contrast *one* with *won*. Discuss the meaning and spelling differences. Connect *come* and *some* and highlight the *o_e* spelling for the /u/ sound.

Extension: Write and have children copy and complete sentence starters, such as:
I have one ___. I once ___.

High-Frequency Words

Name: _____ Date: _____

High-Frequency Hurdles #3

	Read It	Mark It	Write It
1.	do	do	
2.	who	who	
3.	to	to	
4.	too	too	
5.	two	two	

Tip: Connect *to*, *do*, and *who*. Discuss the confusion with *go*, *no*, and *so*—words many children learn early on. Contrast *to* with *two* and *too*. Discuss the different spellings and meanings.

Extension: Write and have children copy and complete sentence starters, such as: *I went to ___. I have two ___. Who is ___?*

Name: _____ Date: _____

High-Frequency Hurdles #4

Read It	Mark It	Write It
1. today	today	
2. together	together	
3. through	through	
4. really	really	
5. eyes	eyes	

Tip: Have children circle *to* in *today* and *together*.

Extension: Write and have children copy and complete sentence starters, such as: *Together we can ___. Today I will ___.*

High-Frequency Words

Name: _____ Date: _____

High-Frequency Hurdles #5

	Read It	Mark It	Write It
1.	of	of	
2.	from	from	
3.	for	for	
4.	four	four	
5.	before	before	

Tip: Contrast *for* with *four*. Discuss the different spellings and meanings. Have children create exemplar sentences for *of*, *for*, and *from* to connect to meaning and usage.

Extension: Write and have children copy and complete sentence starters, such as:
I am from ___. I ___ before I go to school. I have a lot of ___.

Name: _____ Date: _____

High-Frequency Hurdles #6

Read It	Mark It	Write It
1. have	have	
2. give	give	
3. live	live	
4. love	love	
5. above	above	

Tip: No English words end in the letter **v**. If you hear the /v/ sound at the end, you must add an **e**. Connect to other words such as *love, glove, above, gave, save*.

Extension: Write and have children copy and complete sentence starters, such as: *We have to ___. I love to ___. Please give me a ___.*

High-Frequency Words

Name: _____ Date: _____

High-Frequency Hurdles #7

Read It	Mark It	Write It
1. you	you	
2. your	your	
3. you're	you're	
4. its	its	
5. it's	it's	

Tip: Contrast *your/you're* and *its/it's*. Discuss the different spellings and meanings.

Extension: Write and have children copy and complete sentence starters, such as:
Your ___ is ___. You're a ___. The ___ hurt its ___. It's fun to ___.

Name: _____   Date: _____

High-Frequency Hurdles #8

Read It	Mark It	Write It
1. they're	they're	
2. their	their	
3. there	there	
4. where	where	
5. wear	wear	

Tip: Contrast *their/there/they're*. Discuss the different spellings and meanings. Connect *there* and *where* and their shared spelling pattern *-ere*.

Extension: Write and have children copy and complete sentence starters, such as:
Where is the ___? There is a ___. Their dog is ___. They're happy to ___.

High-Frequency Words

Name: _____ Date: _____

High-Frequency Hurdles #9

Read It	Mark It	Write It
1. the	the	
2. them	them	
3. then	then	
4. when	when	
5. whenever	whenever	

Tip: Words that begin with **th** and **wh** can cause challenges when reading and spelling, especially when they vary only slightly (e.g., **then/when, that/what**). Do lots of word-building activities with these words and have children create high-frequency word phrase cards to practice reading.

Extension: Write and have children copy and complete sentence starters, such as:
When do we ___? Tell them that ___. The ___ is ___. I ___ whenever I'm happy.

Name: _____ Date: _____

High-Frequency Hurdles #10

Read It	Mark It	Write It
1. what	what	
2. that	that	
3. this	this	
4. with	with	
5. who	who	

Tip: Words that begin with **th** and **wh** can cause challenges when reading and spelling, especially when they vary only slightly (e.g., **then/when, that/what**). Do lots of word-building activities with these words and have children create high-frequency word phrase cards to practice reading.

Extension: Write and have children copy and complete sentence starters, such as:
Who is ___? This is a ___. I will go with ___ to the ___. What can you ___?

High-Frequency Words

Name: _____ Date: _____

High-Frequency Hurdles #11

Read It	Mark It	Write It
1. don't	don't	
2. won't	won't	
3. most	most	
4. both	both	
5. also	also	

Tip: Connect **don't** (*do not*) and **won't** (*will not*). Point out the letter **o** for the **long-o** sound.

Extension: Write and have children copy and complete sentence starters, such as:
I don't have ___. I won't ___! Most of my friends ___. I have both a ___ and a ___.

Name: _____   Date: _____

High-Frequency Hurdles #12

Read It	Mark It	Write It
1. saw	saw	
2. was	was	
3. on	on	
4. no	no	
5. know	know	

Tip: Discuss reversals *was/saw* and *on/no*. Highlight *a* for /u/ and *s* for /z/ in *was* and compare to *is* and *has*. Contrast *no* with *know*. Discuss the different spellings and meanings.

Extension: Write and have children copy and complete sentence starters, such as:
I know how to ___. I saw a ___. The ___ was ___.

High-Frequency Words

Name: _____ Date: _____

High-Frequency Hurdles #13

	Read It	Mark It	Write It
1.	word	word	
2.	work	work	
3.	wash	wash	
4.	water	water	
5.	want	want	

Tip: Focus on words that begin with *wa-* and how to pronounce the vowel sound. Explain that the *-or* spelling in *word* and *work* stands for the /ûr/ sounds.

Extension: Write and have children copy and complete sentence starters, such as:
My favorite word is ___. Put water in ___. I want to ___

High-Frequency Words

Name: _____ Date: _____

High-Frequency Hurdles #14

Read It	Mark It	Write It
1. said	said	
2. they	they	
3. been	been	
4. again	again	
5. does	does	

Tip: Highlight specific sound-spellings that are frequently misspelled, such as *ai* for /e/ in *said* and *again*, and *ey* for /ā/ in *they*. Highlight the initial schwa sound for *a* in *again*. Highlight the *oe* spelling for /u/ in *does* (and connect to *do*). Contrast with *goes*. Point out *does* = *do* + *es*; *goes* = *go* + *es*.

Extension: Write and have children copy and complete sentence starters, such as:
They can ___. I have been ___. I want to ___ again. My teacher said to ___.

The Megabook of Spelling: Grades K–2 © Wiley Blevins, Scholastic Inc.

High-Frequency Words

Name: _____   Date: _____

High-Frequency Hurdles #15

Read It	Mark It	Write It
1. put	put	
2. push	push	
3. pull	pull	
4. buy	buy	
5. why	why	

Tip: Contrast **buy** with **by** (like *why, cry, try*) and **bye** (from *God be with ye*—an old way to say "goodbye"). Discuss the different spellings and meanings.

Extension: Write and have children copy and complete sentence starters, such as:
Please put the ___ in the ___. Why are you ___? I want to buy a ___.

Name: _____   Date: _____

High-Frequency Hurdles #16

Read It	Mark It	Write It
1. any	any	
2. many	many	
3. carry	carry	
4. very	very	
5. every	every	

Tip: Connect *any* and *many*. Highlight the /ē/ sound spelled *y* at the ends of these words. Point out the *e* in the middle of *every*, which most people do not pronounce (/evrē/) and is likely to be missing from children's spellings.

Extension: Write and have children copy and complete sentence starters, such as:
I have many ___. I can carry a ___. I am very ___.

High-Frequency Words

Name: _____ Date: _____

High-Frequency Hurdles #17

Read It	Mark It	Write It
1. pretty	pretty	
2. people	people	
3. because	because	
4. eight	eight	
5. laugh	laugh	

Tip: This is an especially difficult group of words for children to master in spelling. Focus on the irregular or challenging parts of each word.

Extension: Write and have children copy and complete sentence starters, such as:
Many people ___. I see eight ___. ___ makes me laugh.

Name: _____   Date: _____

High-Frequency Hurdles #18

Read It	Mark It	Write It
1. different	different	
2. other	other	
3. are	are	
4. were	were	
5. we're	we're	

Tip: Highlight specific sound-spellings that are frequently misspelled, such as the *e* in the middle of **different**, which most people do not pronounce (/difrunt/) and is likely to be missing from children's spellings.

Extension: Write and have children copy and complete sentence starters, such as:
A ___ is different from a ___. Are you ___? We're going to ___.

High-Frequency Words

High-Frequency Hurdles #19

Read It	Mark It	Write It
1. earth	earth	
2. world	world	
3. children	children	
4. mother	mother	
5. father	father	

Tip: This is an especially difficult group of words for children to master in spelling. Focus on the irregular or challenging parts of each word.

Extension: Write and have children copy and complete sentence starters, such as:
Many children ___. The earth is ___. My mother/father can ___.

Name: _____ Date: _____

High-Frequency Hurdles #20

Read It	Mark It	Write It
1. answer	answer	
2. question	question	
3. another	another	
4. sentence	sentence	
5. animal	animal	

Tip: Highlight specific sound-spellings that are frequently misspelled, such as the **w** in *answer*, which is silent (etymology = I **sw**ear to tell the truth), and the **-tion** ending of *question*.

Extension: Write and have children copy and complete sentence starters, such as: *My favorite animal is ___. I need another ___. I will write a sentence about ___.*

High-Frequency Words

Name: _____   Date: _____

High-Frequency Hurdles #21

Read It	Mark It	Write It
1. great	great	
2. picture	picture	
3. country	country	
4. mountain	mountain	
5. enough	enough	

Tip: Highlight specific sound-spellings that are frequently misspelled, such as the *ea* spelling for the **long-a** sound in *great*, the *-tain* ending in **mountain**, the *-ture* ending in **picture**, and the *-ough* ending in **enough**.

Extension: Write and have children copy and complete sentence starters, such as:
It feels great when ___. I have had enough ___. My country is ___.

High-Frequency Word Map It

Section 11

Irregular High-Frequency Words

High-Frequency Words

Name: _____ Date: _____

Map It!

Say It	Count It
💬	○ ○ ○ ○ ○

Map It

Spell It (add ♥)

Write It

To the teacher: Say a high-frequency word and have children repeat. Then, have them count (tap) the sounds as they point to each circle. Next, have them map each sound onto a box by marking each box with a dot. After that, have them spell the word by writing a letter or spelling in each box. Guide children to add a heart above any challenging spellings. Finally, have them write each word two times in their best handwriting.

High-Frequency Words

Name: _____   Date: _____

Map It!

Say It	Count It
	○ ○ ○ ○ ○

Map It				

Spell It (add ♥)				

Write It	

SECTION 12

Handwriting Fluency

For children to spell well, they must learn the most frequent spellings for each sound in English. This is accomplished through explicit phonics instruction in the first few years of school. At the same time, children need to develop handwriting fluency—the automatic formation of letters. Activities in kindergarten (and beyond as needed) in which children practice writing the letters of the alphabet as they say each letter's most common sound can accelerate and solidify this learning. Teachers typically review letter-sounds briefly at the beginnings of lessons using letter and spelling cards. Children see the letter or spelling and chorally state the sound. The reverse should also happen as a daily warm-up. The teacher should say a sound and ask children to write the letter or spelling (sometimes multiple spellings) for that sound. The teacher can reinforce proper letter formation during this activity. Some children struggle with where to start forming a letter and how to correctly form it.

Handwriting Fluency: A Warm-Up Routine

Research shows the importance of handwriting fluency and its impact on the quantity, content, and quality of children's writing. In addition to modeling letter formation (e.g., where to start each letter, how to grip the pencil, proper writing posture) and having children practice writing the letters/spellings as they say the associated sound, begin each phonics lesson with a fluency warm-up. This should take no more than 3–4 minutes. Do the following:

- Display letter or spelling cards for the taught phonics skills. Display or point to each one in quick succession as children say the associated sound or sounds. Take note of errors and provide corrective feedback.
- Next, say a sound and have children write the letter or spelling(s) on a dry-erase board. Circulate and observe. Write the correct letter or spelling on the board for children to self-check. This is an ideal moment to model letter formation as needed and to provide articulation support for similar sounds that might be causing some children confusion.

Materials Needed	The following pages provide guided practice in handwriting. • Pages 292–301 feature handwriting practice pages organized by common letter strokes. • Pages 302–309 provide handwriting templates for lowercase letters. • Page 310 offers a handwriting assessment. • Pages 311–314 focus on handwriting practice with high-frequency words. **Optional** (from your phonics program): • sound-spelling cards • articulation videos
Length of Activity	5 minutes
Location	school or home

Principle 2: Phonics and Handwriting Fluency

Skills Practiced

Phonemic Awareness

Handwriting

Spelling

Decoding

Dictation

Writing

Section 12 downloadables are available here.

Section 12

Handwriting Fluency

Handwriting Routine

Routine Steps	Sample Teacher Talk
Step 1: Review Letter Name, Sound, and Articulatory Gestures Use a sound-spelling card (from your phonics program) to review the letter name, sound, and key word. Use an articulation video (also from your phonics program) to review how to form the sound. Scholastic's *Articulation Cards* feature close-up photos and online videos of children articulating each sound of the English language.	**Lowercase *a*** *Say /a/ as in* **apple**. [Point to the letter on your phonics program's sound-spelling card.] *This is the lowercase letter* **a**. *We write the letter* **a** *for the /a/ sound.* *Let's watch the articulation video for /a/.* [Use a video from your phonics program or one online.] *Now, watch my mouth as I make this sound: /a/. Notice how my mouth is open and my lips are far apart. Everyone say: /a/. Now watch your partner say /a/. What do you notice about your mouth?*
Step 2: Engage Through Multisensory Experiences Play a letter video (from your phonics program). Have children stand and perform the handwriting actions.	*Let's watch the letter* **Aa** *video.* [Use a video from your phonics program or one online.] *Everyone stand and join in with the song and handwriting motions.*
Step 3: Review Key Letter Strokes Provide practice with the key strokes used to form each letter, such as circles, straight lines, and diagonals.	*We use two handwriting strokes to write the lowercase* **a**. *We use a circle and a straight line. Let's practice writing circles. Watch as I model. I start on the black dot, then circle back and around.* *Now, you try. Put your pencil on the black dot. Circle back and around. When you are finished, write four or five more circles.* *Let's also practice writing straight lines. Watch as I model. I start on the black dot, then pull straight down to the ground (bottom line).* *Now, you try. Put your pencil on the black dot. Pull straight down to the ground line. When you are finished, write four or five more straight lines.*

Routine Steps (continued)	Sample Teacher Talk (continued)
Step 4: Model Letter Formation Use a handwriting chant to teach and model how to form the letter. Match the timing of your speech with the action of modeling the letter formation. Focus on where to start each letter using the black dots. Use any visual supports provided on the lines as needed, including the ground/bottom line, the middle line, the sky/top line, and going underground. Have children repeat the chant when practicing how to form the letter at the beginning. Repeat the chant frequently when providing corrective feedback.	*Now, let's write a lowercase letter **a**. Watch as I model.* *I start at the black dot. Then I circle back, lift, and pull down to the ground.* *Now, watch as I write the lowercase letter **a** two more times. Say the chant with me as I write the letter:* Circle back, lift, and pull down to the ground. Circle back, lift, and pull down to the ground. **Note:** For easy reference, some teachers refer to TALL letters (reach the top line), SMALL letters (appear between the middle and bottom line), and FALL letters (dip below the bottom line).
Step 5: Guide Practice Have children write the letter four to six times on the line. Note that practice pages should provide a model with directional arrows, traceable gray letters, and plenty of space for children to write the letter on their own. Have children say the letter sound as they write the letter each time. When completed, have children circle their best effort in each row.	*It's your turn. Look at the gray lowercase letter **a**. Do you see the arrows reminding you how to form the letter?* *Now, trace the gray letter. Place your pencil on the black dot to start. Say the chant with me as you trace the letter:* Circle back, lift, and pull down to the ground. *Write four or five more lowercase letter **a**'s on your own.* *When you're done, circle your best effort on each row.*
Step 6: Build Handwriting Fluency On subsequent days, provide a review warm-up. Show a letter card for the new skill and review skills. Have children chorally say the sound. Then say the sound for the new skill and review skills. Have children write the letter on paper or dry-erase boards. Provide corrective feedback by modeling using a handwriting chant. Offer articulation support for children who confuse similar letter-sounds.	*Time for our phonics warm-up. Look at the letter cards as I show them. Say the sound for each letter, nice and loud.* [Use letter cards for ***a*** and previously taught letter-sounds.] *Now, get out your dry-erase boards. I will say a sound. I want you to write the letter for the sound. Are you ready? Write the letter for /a/.* [Circulate and take note of errors. Model on the board as needed, especially if children start the letter in the incorrect place or struggle with specific writing strokes. You might also need to model articulation—how to form the sound—if children confuse letters with similar sounds.] *Write the letter for…* [Continue with other sounds for letters previously taught.]

Section 12

Handwriting Fluency

Section 12

Handwriting Fluency

Routine Steps (continued)	Sample Teacher Talk (continued)
Step 7: Evaluate and Differentiate Use a letter-formation assessment form to assess children's mastery of each letter. Collect three student writing samples or evaluate their most recent written work. On the form, mark any letters for which children need additional modeling and practice. Use the information to determine changes to whole-group work (e.g., adding specific letters to the handwriting fluency warm-up activity) or to form small groups of children who struggle writing specific letters. Use the extra practice pages, guided small-group activities, and center activities to provide additional practice.	[Use a letter-formation assessment form, such as the one on page 310, to evaluate each child's letter mastery and offer follow-up support as needed using the resources provided.]

Handwriting Assessment

Name: _____ Date: _____

Letter-Formation Assessment

Use the Observation Checklist below to formally assess each child's mastery of letter formation.

When to Administer: Administer this assessment three times a year—beginning, middle, and end.

- Letter formation is best assessed by reviewing a child's writing. Collect three samples of the child's work.
- Evaluate the letter formation. On the Observation Checklist below, circle the letters the child forms inconsistently and incorrectly.
- Mark both uppercase and lowercase letters.

Next Steps: Use the results to form small-group handwriting lessons. Model how to write each letter and provide opportunities for children to trace the letter, then practice writing it on paper. Remind children to say the letter's sound when writing the letter. Finally, have children copy and write five to seven words containing the letter.

Observation Checklist

Uppercase Letters					Lowercase Letters				
A	B	C	D	E	a	b	c	d	e
F	G	H	I	J	f	g	h	i	j
K	L	M	N	O	k	l	m	n	o
P	Q	R	S	T	p	q	r	s	t
U	V	W	X	Y Z	u	v	w	x	y z

Handwriting Fluency

Section 12
Handwriting Fluency

Handwriting Fluency

Name: _____ Date: _____

Letters With _____

Listen and Write	Copy and Correct	Practice and Say
1.		
2.		
3.		
4.		

Circle your best letter in each row.

To the teacher: Say a sound and have children write the letter. Write the letter on the board for children to self-correct and/or copy. Ask children to write the letter three more times and circle their best effort.

Handwriting Fluency

Name: _____   Date: _____

Letters With _____

Listen and Write	Copy and Correct	Practice and Say
1.		
2.		
3.		
4.		

Circle your best letter in each row.

Handwriting Fluency

Name: _____ Date: _____

Uppercase Letters With Sticks

Trace	Write	Practice and Say
1.		
2.		
3.		
4.		

Circle your best letter in each row.

Handwriting Fluency

Name: _____ Date: _____

Uppercase Letters With Sticks

Trace	Copy and Correct	Practice and Say
1.		
2.		
3.		
4.		

Circle your best letter in each row.

Handwriting Fluency

Name: _____ Date: _____

Uppercase Letters With Curves

Trace	Copy and Correct	Practice and Say
1.		
2.		
3.		
4.		

Circle your best letter in each row.

Handwriting Fluency

Name: _____   Date: _____

Uppercase Letters With Curves

Trace	Write	Practice and Say
1. S		
2. G		
3. Q		
4. C		

Circle your best letter in each row.

Handwriting Fluency

Name: _____ Date: _____

Uppercase Letters With Sticks and Curves

Trace	Write	Practice and Say
1. D		
2. B		
3. P		
4. U		

Circle your best letter in each row.

Handwriting Fluency

Name: _____ Date: _____

Uppercase Letters With Sticks and Curves

Trace	Write	Practice and Say
1. U		
2. J		
3. B		
4. P		

Circle your best letter in each row.

Handwriting Fluency

Name: _____ Date: _____

Uppercase Letters With Diagonals

Trace	Write	Practice and Say
1. X		
2. V		
3. W		
4. Y		

Circle your best letter in each row.

The Megabook of Spelling: Grades K–2 © Wiley Blevins, Scholastic Inc.

Handwriting Fluency

Name: _____ Date: _____

Uppercase Letters With Diagonals

Trace	Write	Practice and Say
1. N		
2. M		
3. W		
4. X		

Circle your best letter in each row.

Handwriting Fluency

Name: _____   Date: _____

Uppercase Letters With Diagonals

Trace	Write	Practice and Say
1. R		
2. A		
3. K		
4. Z		

Circle your best letter in each row.

Handwriting Fluency

Name: _____ Date: _____

Lowercase Letters

Trace	Write	Practice and Say
1.		
2.		
3.		
4.		

Circle your best letter in each row.

Handwriting Fluency

Name: _____ Date: _____

Lowercase Letters

Trace	Write	Practice and Say
1.		
2.		
3.		
4.		

Circle your best letter in each row.

Handwriting Fluency

Name: _____ Date: _____

Lowercase Letters

Trace	Write	Practice and Say
1.		
2.		
3.		
4.		

Circle your best letter in each row.

Handwriting Fluency

Name: _____ Date: _____

Lowercase Letters

Trace	Write	Practice and Say
1.		
2.		
3.		
4.		

Circle your best letter in each row.

The Megabook of Spelling: Grades K–2 © Wiley Blevins, Scholastic Inc.

Handwriting Fluency

Name: _____   Date: _____

Lowercase Letters

Trace	Write	Practice and Say
1. b		
2. d		
3. p		
4. q		

Circle your best letter in each row.

Handwriting Fluency

Name: _____ Date: _____

Lowercase Letters

Trace	Write	Practice and Say
1. g		
2. p		
3. q		
4. y		

Circle your best letter in each row.

Handwriting Fluency

Name: _____   Date: _____

Lowercase Letters

Trace	Write	Practice and Say
1.		
2.		
3.		
4.		

Circle your best letter in each row.

Name: _____ Date: _____

Lowercase Letters

Trace	Write	Practice and Say
1. r		
2. f		
3. y		
4. z		

Circle your best letter in each row.

Handwriting Assessment

Name: _____ Date: _____

Letter-Formation Assessment

Use the Observation Checklist below to formally assess each child's mastery of letter formation.

When to Administer: Administer this assessment three times a year—beginning, middle, and end.

- Letter formation is best assessed by reviewing a child's writing. Collect three samples of the child's work.

- Evaluate the letter formation. On the Observation Checklist below, circle the letters the child forms inconsistently and incorrectly.

- Mark both uppercase and lowercase letters.

Next Steps: Use the results to form small-group handwriting lessons. Model how to write each letter and provide opportunities for children to trace the letter, then practice writing it on paper. Remind children to say the letter's sound when writing the letter. Finally, have children copy and write five to seven words containing the letter.

Observation Checklist

Uppercase Letters					Lowercase Letters				
A	B	C	D	E	a	b	c	d	e
F	G	H	I	J	f	g	h	i	j
K	L	M	N	O	k	l	m	n	o
P	Q	R	S	T	p	q	r	s	t
U	V	W	X	Y	Z	u	v	w	x	y	z

More Handwriting Fluency: Decodable High-Frequency Words

High-frequency words that become decodable at various places in your scope and sequence provide great words for handwriting practice. Writing these words multiple times and in phrases and sentences increases children's mastery of them. Below is a list of decodable high-frequency words you can use for additional handwriting fluency practice. Use the form on page 314 to practice.

Decodable High-Frequency Words

Phonics Skill	Simple Words (Grades K–1; vowel spelling and single consonants)		Complex Words (Grades 1–2; vowel spelling and blends and digraphs)		Multisyllabic Words (Grades 2–3; multisyllabic words)	
Short a	am	had	and	than	after	
	an	has	ask	that		
	as	man	back			
	at	ran	black			
	can		fast			
Short e	get		best	well	better	open
	let		help	went	even	seven
	red		tell	when	every	yellow
	ten		them		myself	
	yes		then		never	
Short i	big	in	bring	this	different	
	did	is	drink	which	into	
	him	it	its	will	little	
	his	sit	pick	wish		
	if	six	things	with		
			think			
Short o	got	not	long	stop	upon	
	hot	on	off			
Short u	but	up	jump	must	funny	under
	cut	us	just	such	number	upon
	run		much			
s-blends			best	must		
			fast	stop		
			first			
r-blends			bring	green		
			brown	grow		

Section 12
Handwriting Fluency

Phonics Skill	Simple Words (Grades K–1)		Complex Words (Grades 1–2)		Multisyllabic Words (Grades 2–3)	
l-blends			black	place		
			blue	please		
			clean	sleep		
sh			she	wish		
ch, tch			each	such		
			much	which		
wh			when	white		
			which	why		
th			than	things		
			thank	think		
			that	this		
			them	those		
			then	three		
			these	with		
ng, nk	long		bring	things		
	sing		drink	think		
			thank			
3-letter blends			three	street		
Soft c	face		place			
Soft g	age	page				
Final e	ate	make	place			
	came	ride	these			
	five	same	those			
	gave	take	used			
	like	time	white			
	made	use	write			
Long a	day	say	play		always	
	may	way			away	
Long e	be	me	clean	she	any	every
	eat	read	each	sleep	because	funny
	he	see	green	three	before	only
	keep	we	here*	years*	even	
			please			
			(* Long-e sound with r, but not r-controlled)			

312   The Megabook of Spelling: Grades K–2

Section 12
Handwriting Fluency

Phonics Skill	Simple Words (Grades K–1)	Complex Words (Grades 1–2)	Multisyllabic Words (Grades 2–3)
Long *i*	by, my, light, right	find, try, fly, why, kind	myself
Long *o*	go, no, own, so	cold, know, goes, old, grow, show, hold	also, open, going, over, only, yellow
Long *u*	cute, use, few		
r*-controlled vowel *ar	far, part	start	
r*-controlled vowel *or	for, or, more		before
r*-controlled vowels *er, ir, ur	her, hurt	first	after, never, another, number, better, over, different, under, every
r*-controlled vowels *are, ear	care, bear	share	
Long *oo*	new, too, soon	blue	into
Short *oo*	good, look	full, pull	
Diphthong *oi, oy*	boy, toy	boil	
Diphthong *ou, ow*	down, our, how, out, now	brown, found, round	about, around
Variant Vowel /ô/	all, fall, call, saw	called, small, draw, walk	also, because, always
silent letters		know, write	
schwa			about, around, another, away

Handwriting Fluency

Name: _____ Date: _____

Decodable High-Frequency Words

Read It	Write It	Write It Again
1.		
2.		
3.		
4.		
5.		

SECTION 13

Rules and Generalizations

There are languages, like Spanish, that we refer to as more "transparent." That means there is a high degree of consistency between the letter and the sound it represents. However, English is a language that is less transparent. We refer to it as an "opaque" language. While there are many letters and spellings that consistently stand for a sound, there are sounds in English that can be represented by many letters or spellings. For example, we can write *e, ee, ea, ie, ei, y,* and *ey* for the long-*e* sound. This opaqueness requires us to spend MORE time for instruction and practice on these spellings with our students and MORE attention to when and why these spellings are used in words. So, effective spelling instruction includes observations, discussions, and explicit explanations about how English words work.

While teaching a vast array of rules is <u>not</u> helpful, there are a handful of rules and generalizations (e.g., no English words end in the letter *v* so you must add an *e*) that are worth teaching children. In addition, deeper focus on related words can reveal the morphophonemic quality of English and how spellings are maintained across related words. For example, the related words *sign, signal,* and *signature,* which all contain "sign," help children understand why that "silent" *g* is necessary in the word *sign*.

Also, some children speak a variation of mainstream English (e.g., African American English, Chicano English) or a regional dialect that pose some complexities when children are spelling words due to modified or dropped sounds. All these require direct instruction and support. Whenever you engage children in spelling and/or dictation activities, clearly and purely articulate words to highlight their sounds and spellings (e.g., *Wed-nes-day*; overemphasize the final blend in a word like *sent*).

Materials Needed	The following pages provide guided practice in assisting children who speak English as an additional language or speak an English variant or dialect. • Page 316 focuses on common rules and generalizations to share with children during instruction to help them better understand how English works. • Pages 317–320 offer supports for children who speak an English variant or dialect.
Length of Activity	n/a
Location	school or home

Principle 5: Focus on How English Works

Skills Practiced

Phonemic Awareness ✓

Handwriting ☐

Spelling ✓

Decoding ✓

Dictation ☐

Writing ☐

Section 13
Rules and Generalizations

Common Phonics Rules and Generalizations Worth Teaching

There are only a handful of spelling generalizations that are truly useful to teach children to help them spell words, but many are related to "irregular" high-frequency words, which can pose challenges for children. Below is a list of the most common rules/generalizations that are worthwhile to teach formally.

Useful Rules and Generalizations

1. English words don't end in the letter *v*. You must add an *e* to any word ending in the /v/ sound (e.g., *have, give, gave, love*).
2. English words don't end in the letter *j*. You must use *ge* or *dge* (e.g., *large, fudge*).
3. English words don't end in *i* or *u* (unless foreign words or clipped words, such as *tofu, ski, flu/influenza, taxi/taxicab*).
4. The position of spellings in words matters (e.g., long *a*: *ai* never appears at the end of a word, but *ay* does).
5. FLSZ/Floss Rule (These letters are doubled after a short vowel: *stiff, well, kiss, jazz*)
6. *c* and *g* before *e, i,* or *y* (e.g., *city, germ*; exception: *girl*)
7. *q* is followed by *u* (e.g., *quick*)
8. *y* at the beginning is a consonant (e.g., *yes*); *y* at the end is a vowel (e.g., *fly, happy*)
9. *z* never spells /s/, but the /z/ sound can be spelled as *s* at the end of some words (e.g., *was, is, has, dogs*)
10. *ck* and *tch* after short vowel (e.g., *sick, catch*); otherwise, it's *k* and *ch* (e.g., *park, lunch*)
11. *augh, eigh, igh, ough* (Phonograms at ends of words or followed by a letter *t*; the *gh* is silent or stands for the /f/ sound; in Old English the silent *gh* was pronounced as /kh/.)

The Many Uses of *e* in English Spelling

1. **hop/hope** (Long vowel sound—vowel says its name)
2. **have/give/love** (No English words end in *v*, so must add *e*)
3. **clue** (No English words end in *u* or *i* unless a clipped word, like *taxi* [for *taxicab*] or a foreign word, like *ski*. Note: This also helps explain why spellings like *ay* and *oy* are at the ends of words while *ai* and *oi* are in the middle—the *i* is replaced by *y*.)
4. **hug/huge** (Soft sound /j/ and no English words end in the letter *j*)
5. **race/nice** (Soft sound /s/ for *c*)
6. **table** (ta/ble—every syllable must have a written vowel letter)
7. **bath/bathe** (Changes unvoiced sound of *th* to voiced sound)
8. **please/house** (Clarifies that the word is not a plural, as in *pleas* vs. *please*. We call that a suffix-canceling *e*.)
9. **are/owe/awe/ewe** (To make a word look bigger)

Other Teaching Points

1. **Inflectional suffixes** change the form of a word but NOT its part of speech.
   -s, -ed, -ing
2. **Derivational suffixes** can change the part of speech.
   govern (verb) → *government* (noun)
3. **Suffix-canceling markers** make it clear that a complete content word is not a plural or help distinguish word meanings.
   pleas/please, bras/brass (FLSZ rule), *cares/caress*

   Note: This does not apply to non-content words, such as *is/was/us/this*, and some foreign or clipped words, such as *bus/buses* (from *omnibus*), and does not apply to suffixes, such as *-less* (*needless* instead of *needles*).

English Dialects

Below are some common sound-spelling variations to address during phonics and spelling activities for children who speak different dialects or variations of English.

African American English (AAE) Phonics Differences

English/Language Arts Skill	Linguistic Differences and Instructional Modifications
Digraph *th*, as in *bathroom*	For many speakers of African American English, the initial /th/ sound in function words, such as *this* and *then*, is often produced as a /d/ sound. In some words, such as *thing* and *through*, the /th/ sound is produced as a /t/ sound. At the ends of words and syllables, such as *bathroom*, *teeth*, *mouth*, and *death*, the /th/ sound is replaced by the /f/ sound. In the word *south*, it is replaced by the /t/ sound (*sout'*). This will affect children's spelling and speaking. Children will need articulation support prior to spelling these words.
Final consonant *r*	Many speakers of African American English drop the /r/ sound in words. For example, these children will say *sto'* for *store* or *do'* for *door*. They might also replace it with the /uh/ sound, as in *sista* for *sister*. Clearly pronounce these words, emphasizing the /r/ sound. Have children repeat several times, exaggerating the sound before spelling these words.
***r*-blends**	Many speakers of African American English drop the /r/ sound in words with *r*-blends. For example, these children will say *th'ow* for *throw*. Clearly pronounce these words in the lesson, emphasizing the sounds of the *r*-blend. Have children repeat several times, exaggerating the sound.
Final consonant *l* and final *l*-blends	Many speakers of African American English drop the /l/ sound in words, particularly in words with *-ool* and *-oal* spelling patterns, such as *cool* and *coal*, and when the letter *l* precedes the consonants *p, t*, or *k*, as in *help*, *belt*, and *milk*. The /l/ sound might also be dropped when it precedes /w/, /j/, /r/ (*a'ready/already*); /u/, /o/, /aw/ (*poo/pool*), or in contractions with *will* (*he'/he'll*). These children will drop the *l* when spelling these words, as well. Provide additional articulation support prior to reading and spelling these words.
Final consonant blends (when both are voiced, as in *ld*, or voiceless, as in *sk*)	Many speakers of African American English drop the final letter in a consonant blend (e.g., *ld, lk, lt, mp, nd, nk, nt, pt, sk, sp, st*) or consonant blend sounds formed when adding *-ed* (e.g., /st/ as in *missed* or /pt/ as in *stopped*). For example, they will say *des'* for *desk*. Clearly pronounce the final sounds in these words and have children repeat several times, exaggerating the sound.
Other final consonants	Many speakers of African American English drop the final consonant in a word when the consonant blend precedes a consonant, as in *bes' kind* for *best kind*. They also drop the final consonant sound in words ending in *-ed*, as in *rub* for *rubbed*. Provide additional articulation support prior to reading and spelling these words.
Plurals	When the letter *s* is added to a word ending in a consonant blend, such as *test* (*tests*), many speakers of African American English will drop the final sound. This is due to the phonological (pronunciation) rules of AAE that restrict final consonant blends. Therefore, they will say *tes'* or *tesses*. These children will need additional articulation support.

Section 13

Rules and Generalizations

African American English (AAE) Phonics Differences (continued)

English/Language Arts Skill	Linguistic Differences and Instructional Modifications
Contractions	Many speakers of African American English drop the /t/ sound when pronouncing the common words *it's*, *that's*, and *what's*. These words will sound more like *i's*, *tha's*, and *wha's*. These children will need additional articulation support to pronounce and spell these words.
Short vowels *i* and *e*	When the /i/ and /e/ sounds appear before the consonants *m* or *n* in words such as *pen/pin* and *him/hem*, many speakers of African American English won't pronounce or hear the difference. Focus on articulation, such as mouth position for each vowel sound, during lessons.
Inflectional ending -*ing*	Many speakers of African American English will pronounce words with -*ing* as /ang/. For example, they will say *thang* for *thing*. Emphasize the /i/ sound in these words to help children correctly spell and pronounce them.
Stress patterns	Many speakers of African American English place the stress on the first syllable in two-syllable words instead of the second syllable (more common in Mainstream English). For example, they will say *po'lite* instead of *polite*. These children will need additional articulation support to pronounce these words.
Homophones	Due to the phonological rules of AAE, many words that are not homophones in Mainstream English become homophones in African American English. This will affect children's spelling and understanding of these words. Some examples include *find/fine*, *run/rung*, *mask/mass*, *pin/pen*, *coal/cold*, *mold/mole*. Focus on articulation, such as mouth position, and differences in meaning for each word pair during lessons.

Chicano/a English (CE) Phonics Differences

English/Language Arts Skill	Linguistic Differences and Instructional Modifications
Final consonants	Many speakers of Chicano English will drop sounds in words or syllables that end with multiple final consonants, thereby reducing the consonant cluster sound to one consonant sound. For example, they will say *mine* instead of *mind* or *harware* for *hardware*. This occurs when consonant clusters are voiced and unvoiced, as in *prized/price*, *worst/worse*, and *strict/strick*. Other consonant clusters that are problematic include *ft*, *sk*, *sp*, and *pt*. This will affect children's spelling and speaking. Children will need articulation support prior to spelling these words. Clearly pronounce these words. Have children repeat them several times, exaggerating the final consonant sounds before spelling these words.
Digraphs /ch/ and /sh/	Many speakers of Chicano English will switch (or merge) the /ch/ and /sh/ sounds. This is more common in Tejanos (Chicanos from Texas) than Californios. Some examples include *teacher/teasher*, *watch/wash*, *chop/shop*, *chair/share*, *shake/chake*, *shy/chy*, *shame/chame*. Provide articulation support. Exaggerate the sound and have children repeat.

Chicano/a English (CE) Phonics Differences (continued)

English/Language Arts Skill	Linguistic Differences and Instructional Modifications
Consonants /z/ and /v/	Many speakers of Chicano English will replace the /z/ sound with /s/ and the /v/ sound with /f/. Examples include *prized/price, fuzz/fuss, raise/race (When I don't race my hand the teasher makes a fuzz)*, and *lives/lifes, save/safe (The hero safe many lifes)*. Articulation support connected to word meanings will be beneficial.
Homophones	Because of the unique phonological rules of Chicano English, many words that are not homophones in Mainstream English will sound like homophones. For example, *fine* will be used for both *fine* and *find*, *tin* will be used for both *tin* and *ten*, and *pen* will be used for both *pen* and *pin*. Clearly pronounce these words and focus on mouth position during articulation. Have children repeat several times, exaggerating the sound before spelling these words.
Stress patterns	In Chicano English, stress is placed on one-syllable prefixes as well as roots. The stress is also often elongated. For example, speakers of Chicano English will say *tooday* for *today*, *deecide* for *decide*, and *reepeat* for *repeat*. Articulation work will be needed.
Intonation	Many speakers of Chicano English will exhibit a pattern of intonation that is different from Mainstream English. This pattern, derived from the Náhuatl language, involves a rise and sustain (or rise and fall) at the end of a phrase or sentence. For example, these speakers will say, "Doont be baaad." Provide articulation support. Recast children's sentences to emphasize intonation when working with children one-on-one.
Consonant /w/	Many speakers of Chicano English will pronounce the /w/ sound with an added breath so that it sounds more like /wh/. As a result, words like *with* sound like *whith* and *will* like *whill*. This might also affect children's spelling. Contrast words beginning with *w* and *wh* and have children keep lists in their writing notebooks.
Pronouncing *the*	The word *the* is pronounced in Mainstream English with a schwa sound *(thuh)* before a word beginning with a consonant, and a long-*e* sound *(thee)* before a word beginning with a vowel. Many speakers of Chicano English will use the schwa pronunciation for all words. Point out the distinction and usage of each pronunciation.

Section 13

Rules and Generalizations

Regional/Dialect Phonics Differences

English/Language Arts Skill	Linguistic Differences and Instructional Modifications
Short *a*	When the short-*a* sound /a/ is followed by /m/ or /n/ (nasal sounds) or /g/, it can affect the pronunciation of /a/ and make it more challenging to distinguish the sound. Some English speakers will also need extra support distinguishing /a/ and /e/ because they are formed in similar ways and are beside each other on the Vowel Valley Sound Wall chart.
Short *i*	Some children might confuse or have difficulty distinguishing the /i/ and /e/ sounds because of regional dialects. When the /i/ and /e/ sounds appear before the consonants *m* or *n* in words such as *pen/pin* and *him/hem*, many speakers of African American English won't pronounce or hear the difference. Model each sound and focus on articulation of confusing word pairs. Say: *The /i/ sound makes you grin, while the /e/ sound makes you drop your chin.*
Short *o*	In some English dialects, when the letter *o* is followed by the letter *g*, as in *dog* and *log*, the sound for the letter *o* is pronounced more like /ô/ than /o/.
Short *e*	In some regions of the United States, English speakers may pronounce short *e* /e/ as long *a* /ā/. For example, *egg* might be pronounced as *aeg*. These speakers might write long *a* with an *e* and will need extra support.
Long *u* vs. Long *oo*	The *u_e* spelling can stand for the long-*u* sound /ū/ in words like *use* and *cute*, and the long-*oo* sound /oo̅/, as in words like *tube* and *rule*. Point this out to children as they encounter these spellings in their readings. Teach mispronunciation correction (set for variability). Say: *What other sound could this spelling stand for? What else could you try?*
Long *i*	The long-*i* sound /ī/ acts like a diphthong—when making the sound there is movement in the mouth, unlike other long-vowel sounds, like long *a* /ā/ and long *e* /ē/, where the mouth maintains a consistent position. This might cause children to use more letters to spell the sound or struggle spelling this sound. Point this out when modeling articulation.
Diphthongs /ou/ and /oi/	Diphthongs are sounds that glide, or move, in the mouth. Some children might struggle attaching discrete spellings to these sounds. Model articulation and point out the movement in the mouth when making the /ou/ and /oi/ sounds.
Variant Vowel /ô/	In some English dialects, the /ô/ sound has been replaced with the short-*o* sound /o/ in words like *bought* and *caught*. In other dialects, the short-*o* sound /o/ has been replaced with the /ô/ sound in words like *cot* and *dog*. This is known as the "cot-caught" merger.